…ociety of

WOO… …VERS

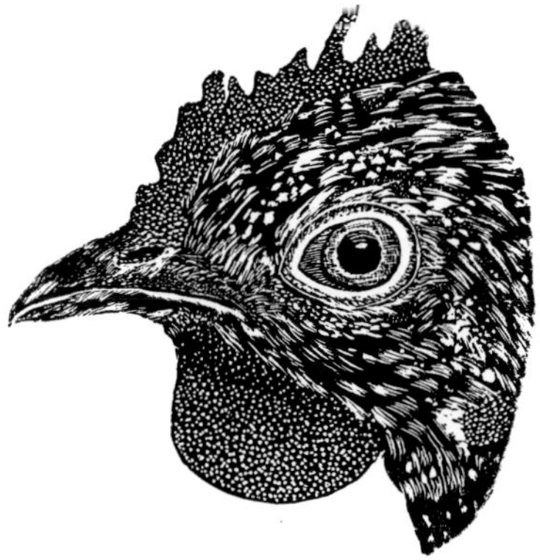

at the time of

THE 66TH ANNUAL EXHIBITION 2003–2004

An illustrated catalogue

Front cover illustration:

Peter Lawrence *Isola Bella, Lake Maggiore* *Catalogue no. 52.*

Title page illustration:

Mary Rossetti Rutterford *And you are?* *Catalogue no. 89.*

ISBN: 0-9546173-0-4

Published by The Society of Wood Engravers

Designed by Oxford Designers & Illustrators www.o-d-i.com
Printed by Hunts, Oxford

CONTENTS

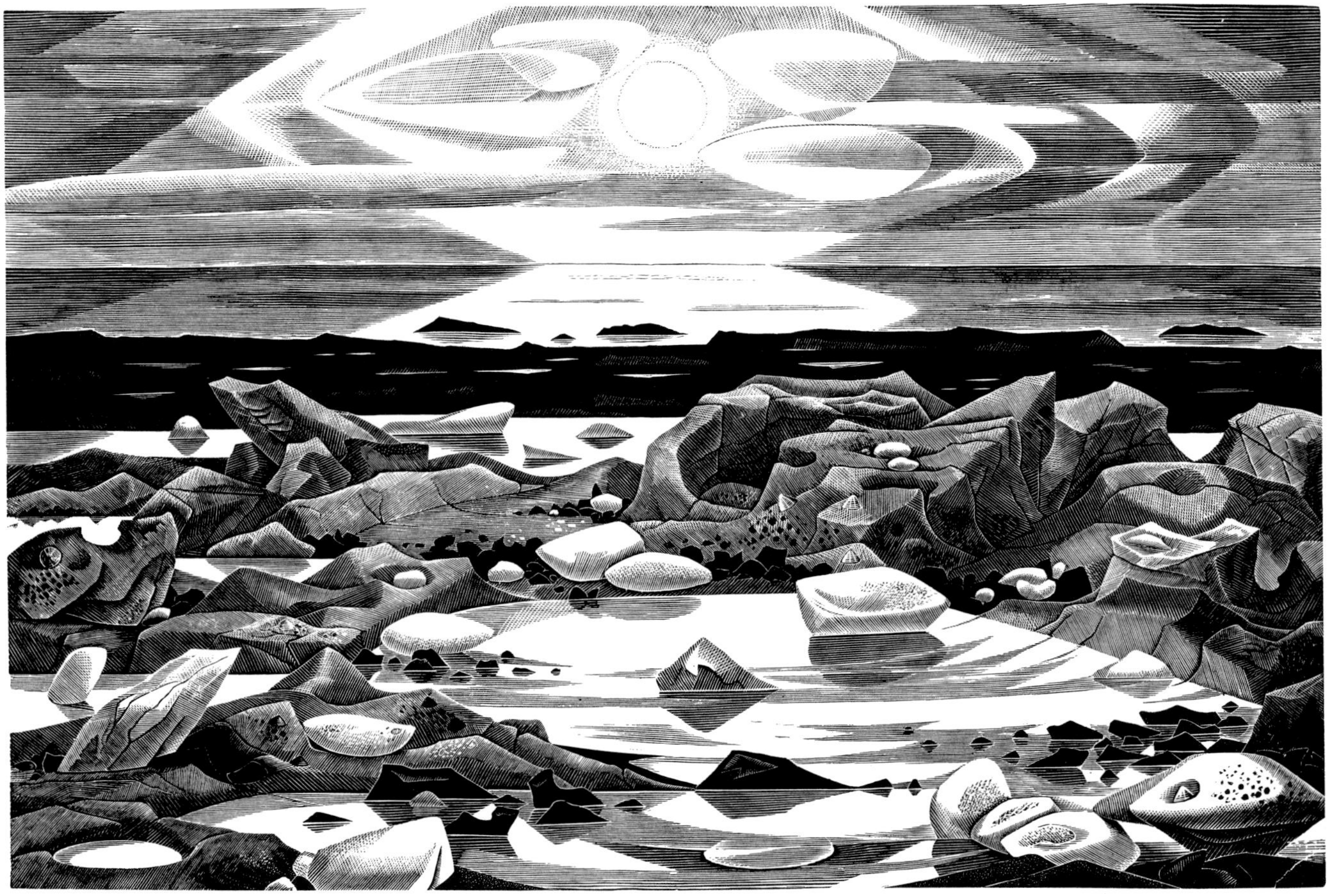

Monica Poole *Chalk Rocks* Catalogue no. 79.

The Society of

FOREWORD

From moribundity in the early eighties to its lively vigour today, the Society of Wood Engravers has evolved over the past twenty years into a highly successful art group. The annual exhibition attracts entries from across the globe and is entirely jury-selected, showing only the best of wood engraving, along with a sprinkling of other relief prints. Visiting six to eight venues each year, the exhibition travels discriminatingly to intimate spaces in remote parts of the UK as well as to prestigious city galleries. This year, an exhibition is also going to South Africa.

In recent years, the SWE has benefited powerfully from the Rawlinson Bequest, which allows us to support the new generation of engravers in training, and the Rachel Reckitt Awards which recognise outstanding work in the annual exhibition. Otherwise, the SWE is entirely self-supporting, relying for its continuing existence on subscriptions, fees and commissions from exhibitions and sales of its publications.

Proceeds from *The Millennium Ark* project, an outstanding collaborative wood engraving which can be seen in the collections of the V & A and Ashmolean museums and of Bristol City Art Gallery, have enabled us to produce this illustrated catalogue. It is the Society's third special catalogue since the revival and it gives some of our more far flung supporters and practitioners an opportunity of 'viewing' the exhibition for the first time. The prints may also be seen on the SWE website.

A significant part of the Society's strength lies in its celebration of links to the past and especially of skills often abandoned elsewhere. We are pleased to hang prints brimming with the freshest ideas from today alongside those acknowledging their debt to the past.

It is a great honour to be associated closely with such an exciting group.

Hilary Paynter
Chairman of the Society of Wood Engravers

www.woodengravers.co.uk

WHAT IS WOOD ENGRAVING?

It is first of all a feeling and in the end a way of thinking – in print.

Many artists experience that visceral first response to one medium above all others which determines their future career; the sound of a cello that makes you think 'I must play that!'; the flooding with colour that makes you respond to paint; the difficulty of paint and the attraction of the clean impression of ink on paper that draws a person to printmaking. Later, as you learn about the thing you fell in love with at first sight, you discover the many aspects which were not revealed in that first impression and realise that your chosen way is also a language, a vehicle, an instrument which requires of you, but also provides for you, its own way of thinking.

In a narrow sense and in a small place between the thinking and the feeling, wood engraving is a technique, a way of making prints first defined for us by Thomas Bewick in the 1790s; its history has been well and frequently rehearsed. But artists do not woo their chosen instrument for the sake of technique or bend its range to new expressiveness in response to history; they do it for love, for now and for the future.

Anyway, 'wood engraving', *now*, encompasses materials and methods beyond the limits of the traditional technique: engraving on woods other than classic box and on materials other than wood. Perspex, Delrin, Resingrave, linoleum and plastic can all be used 'in the spirit of wood engraving'. And one may engrave with tools other than the traditional burins – notably, in some hands, the flexidrive shaft. What unites the work is that feeling, that spirit:

an aesthetic, a way of working which I have defined elsewhere as 'fine relief engraving'. It is worth trying to explain more closely what that means.

ENGRAVING

To engrave is not just to cut marks into a surface, but to do it with a strong implication of precision and purpose. It is to prefer control to accident. It is to love the patterns formed on the surface by the accumulation of small, precisely-made marks as well as the image they create.

The tooling of the surface can stand in considerable creative tension with the making of powerful or expressive imagery; but while many of the smaller, more 'vernacular' images in this exhibition are indeed decorative or elegant in their handling when most resolved, it will also be found that more adventurous work has not only broken open an older prettiness towards new expression but has broken through to a new way of reconciling it with the decorated surface. The artist who wants to hack and jab will soon move on to coarser materials, while materials usually used for a broader approach – lino, side-grain wood or synthetics, which allow for extended sizes – can all be used with an engraver's care.

The artistic problems of printmakers who choose to make notably larger wood engravings are similar to those of the pointillist painter or the tapestry weaver: how to make large images out of tiny strokes without the texture becoming overwhelming or pointlessly laborious. They require the sense of order in design which also characterises the best wood engravers.

RELIEF

Of all the ways of making a print, relief printing is the simplest. It just means a print printed off the top surface of a block. Wood engraving in particular does not need any of the machinery or chemical processes which characterise other methods. Wood engravers tend to focus on what goes into the block, where other printmakers can get quite involved in the technicalities of printing itself.

Because the top surface into which the lines are engraved takes the ink, the lines engraved out of it remain light. The wood engraver draws with light. The lines, dots and directional strokes create *light* in the picture – well, usually. (In every other medium, the drawing tool makes dark marks and therefore basically represents shadow.) So the wood engraver, as well as thinking in terms of flat pattern also thinks like a stage director, conjuring his meanings and his stories out of darkness with the tool of light.

Refined presswork can be brought to bear on the result, of course; but in relief printing, just done in black, as is mostly the case for wood engravings, there tends to be less scope for technical experiment as such, and more for considered meaning.

FINE

The 'fine-ness' or 'finesse' of wood engraving is what finally distinguishes it, even from other forms of relief printmaking. There, the marks can have a powerful urgency; woodcut and linocut lend themselves to broad or even coarse handling. But woodcut used in that way cannot produce a subtle tonal range, let alone the tonal range which is not just associated with wood engraving but which wood engraving itself generates. This is what forms the distinct aesthetic, or ambience of feeling, in which the wood engraver's imagination can roam almost indefinitely.

The scale of the wood engraver's cutting seems to derive from the tools used; but, of course, they were originally evolved to make the marks required – marks at the scale of type; marks which hover at or below the threshold of seeing. Modern extensions of engraving tools into new or mechanised forms only continue what Bewick did in adapting metal engravers' tools for wood.

Close scrutiny of a wood engraving will reveal the patterned surface. At normal range the marks coalesce into areas of rich, subtle, silvery or pewtery tone. Powerful urgency comes from the force of the image itself, the organisation of the design, rather than from the mere force or size of the mark. The medium is capable of the most tender distinctions, in steady grades or in a shimmer of marks, according to their scale.

Because these **fine** marks are **engraved** and because they are printed in **relief**, the tonality is quite distinct from the equally (but differently) rich tonalities of etching or mezzotint. The aesthetic of wood engraving is about the release of light rather than the imposition of darkness. The Society of Wood Engravers exists to sustain and develop this – yes – unique area within the visual repertoire of humanity.

It is not really here for the preservation of a craft; though the practical naturally forms a *sine qua non* at the core of the Society's concerns. The

Society exists for the art and the sensibility it represents. Wherever that sensibility is extended and renewed, by new insights, new methods or new artists, the Society is interested. Wherever in the natural or man-made world, it seems to be foreshadowed, its artists recognise it with something of that first leap of the heart that drew us in.

Many people experience the relation of art and life in this way. A potter, a weaver or an oboeist will see or hear things in the world that seem to have been just made for their particular form of expression; those who love those arts will experience it too and value the artists' articulation of it. Artists often choose or feel chosen by a material or a technique that speaks to them. They choose to work within it rather than break it open, sustaining and prolonging it, both to abide by and to question. It is vital to have both kinds, those artists who consolidate the known and are fascinated by eternal questions – how to make the perfect bowl; how to renew the sonnet – and those who stretch the medium into new forms and new expressions.

Both kinds are represented in this exhibition.

Simon Brett

THE SOCIETY OF WOOD ENGRAVERS

at the time of the 66th Annual Exhibition

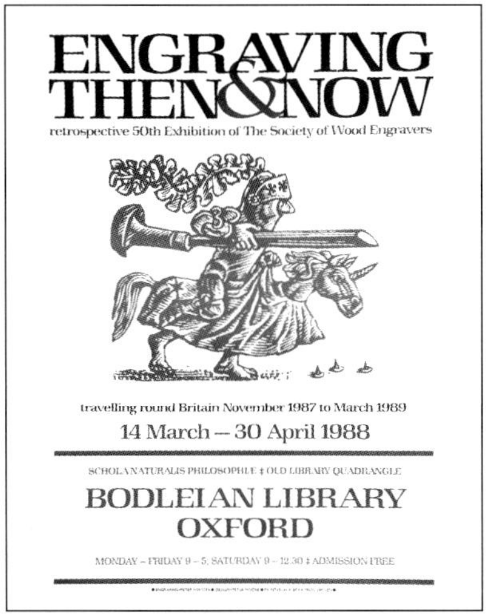

The exhibition for which this is the catalogue is the twentieth since the Society's revival. This is the third illustrated catalogue with a commentary produced in that period. It is a sort of marker. Next year, in 2004, the 'new' society comes of age.

On the occasion of the first catalogue, we set ourselves a challenge. *Engraving Then and Now* (1987), mounted shortly after the re-establishment of the Society, was the fiftieth exhibition since its original foundation in 1920. We showed a work by every member of the past and present Society that we could find, setting major works by present members alongside major works by artists of the 1920s and 1930s to see how they compared. Work by work, they compared well; but it was impossible to know whether, with time, we would stay the course.

Certainly, though, our founders had had fashion on their side; and history (including the history they wrote themselves) had been kind to them. Ours was going to be a tougher row to hoe. The medium which we were seeking to re-invigorate, because we loved it and did not want to see it pass into oblivion, was no longer avant-garde nor likely to be again.

The second major exhibition, *Wood Engraving Here and Now* (1995), featured the work of fifteen members of the Society, and sought an interim answer to the question of artistic stature left open by the first. Three of the artists were American or Canadian; transatlantic contributions had by then greatly changed the profile of the art. The show celebrated the

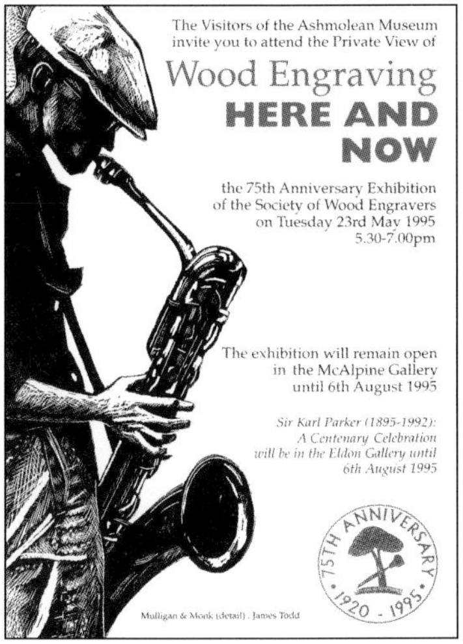

75th anniversary of the Society itself, and was held, by invitation, at the Ashmolean Museum in Oxford. It travelled on to The Gallery in Cork Street, London, and the Whitworth Art Gallery, Manchester. Both public galleries have a long association with wood engraved prints.

This third exhibition for which we have produced an illustrated catalogue is simply the 66th Exhibition of the Society. It has been selected as usual from an open and world-wide submission in which the only right elected members of the Society have over non-members is that they may submit three prints instead of two. All work is subject to selection.

Why then the special catalogue?

It is twenty years since the first exhibition of the revived Society, the 47th of the Society overall, took place at the Garden Gallery in Kew. In October 1984, no one would have assumed that, twenty years on, we would be able to point to an unbroken record of promoting wood engraved printmaking. That is what this exhibition celebrates.

Sales of wood engraved prints are good (better than they ever were in the earlier period with which our revival has naturally been compared). The exhibition pays its way. The Society runs without help from public funding. We regularly tour secondary, themed exhibitions; so there are sometimes two shows on the road at once. Publicly funded galleries up and down the country book the Society's shows, as yet unsubmitted, unselected and unseen, in advance, because the Society's name has become a guarantee. Public galleries

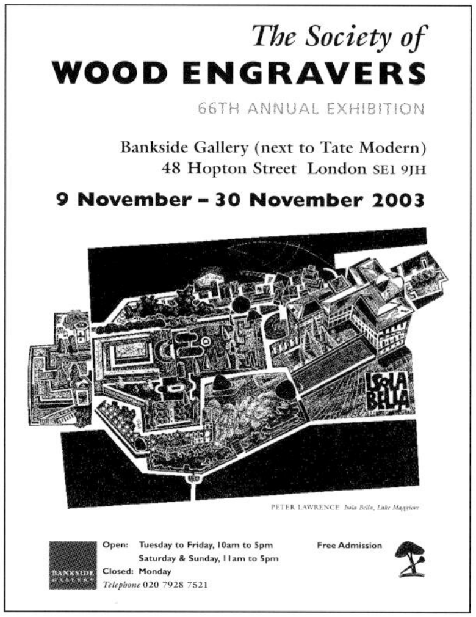

know that we attract good work and select good work; they also know there is a public for it. That this has been the case for some years now is due, firstly and obviously, to the artists themselves and the excellence of their work; but the Society's policy of selection, the insistence not just on quality but on quality control for all, has been fundamental to it.

The revived Society has now outlasted what the artists of the first era themselves called the 'golden age' of wood engraving, the nineteen years between 1920 and the outbreak of World War II. By 1939, our founders were declaring the golden age of wood engraving to be over and began to write their own valedictions. We feel no such inclination. Our gold, we trust, is less perishable.

The Society of Wood Engravers is a British-based artists' exhibiting society first of all. But it has always also been a rallying-point for artists in any country who practise the art and wish to be in touch. An additional, invited International section of 59 prints by a dozen artists, mainly from America and Russia, was a feature of the Bloomsbury Gallery showing of the 48th exhibition (1986), only the second of the revived Society. Overseas artists immediately began to submit work to the annual shows and do so regularly; our most recent discoveries are the wood engravers of Japan and Italy. Partly due to our example, the Wood Engravers' Network began to operate from Ann Arbor, Michigan, putting American and Canadian engravers in touch with each other.

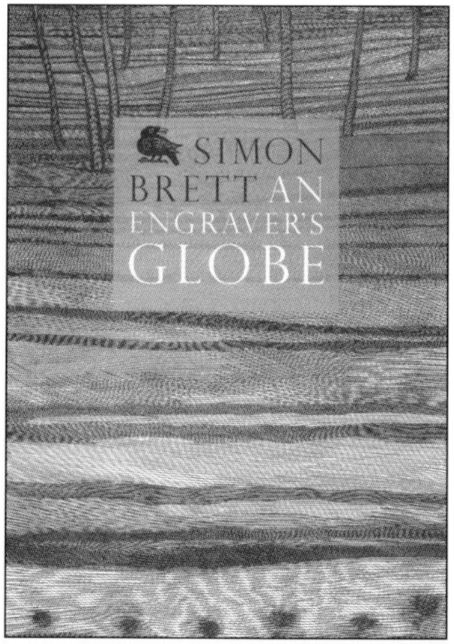

Each new introduction makes the picture of wood engraving around the world more diverse and shows up our own work in a different light. This ever-expanding perception has been chronicled by a sequence of books initiated by the Society, *Engravers* (1987), *Engravers Two* (1992) and the truly international survey *An Engraver's Globe* (2002). British wood engravers are part of a world-wide diaspora. The modernity of much of this work is startling, varied, and unquestionable, though it is not necessarily an engagement with *fashionable* trends. Wood engraving engenders its own way of thinking and feeling, and its own way of being modern, as well as its own way of touching, in 'vernacular' styles, on perennial themes.

This exhibition, starting on Bankside, is one aspect of art in Britain and the world today. The bigger building next door shows... other aspects, merely. The applications of wood engraving – greater than those of most printmaking media – range from fine-art printmaking, 'pure' or in mixed-media works, through illustration in 'fine print' and commercial books, to advertising, packaging and, famously, mural decoration. And not just David Gentleman's at Charing Cross. A new commission for the Newcastle Metro will celebrate this year's 250th anniversary of Thomas Bewick's birth with the work of his very different, quite up-to-the-moment descendants.

Simon Brett

A VIEW FROM JAPAN

Reiko Yamanouchi

The practice of wood engraving in Japan started rather late. It was brought to Japan in 1887 by an artist who had spent six years in France. It was only twenty years after the country was opened to the West in 1868 after three hundred and fifty years of closure. He was one of many artists who were sent to Europe to learn and bring back various techniques of Western arts. He set up a studio of wood engraving and was actively engaged in the art and had a large number of artisans to teach and work with him, and later various artists took it up and produced some work of note.

But it did not become widespread or deep-rooted enough for a long time, and during and after World War II it was almost forgotten. It was a prominent artist Takao Hiwasaki who 'discovered' wood engraving and raised it from oblivion to an important genre of art with his vigorous and startling series of work in the late 1960s and early 1970s. Originally a half-hearted oil painter, and drawn to woodcut and copperplate, he had never had formal training in wood engraving. How he came to find it is a rather dramatic story. One day he was inspired by a poem by Dylan Thomas and wanted to express his semi-religious sense of uplift in art. He had three burins at hand from his copperplate class, but no block, so he rushed to a nearby firewood merchant's and found a log of cherry tree, from which he sawed an inch thick piece and polished its surface. He then engraved on it from morning till night non-stop, and using oil ink, printed it on Tonoko paper with a baren and a spoon. He records how deeply excited and moved he was when he peeled the first sheet

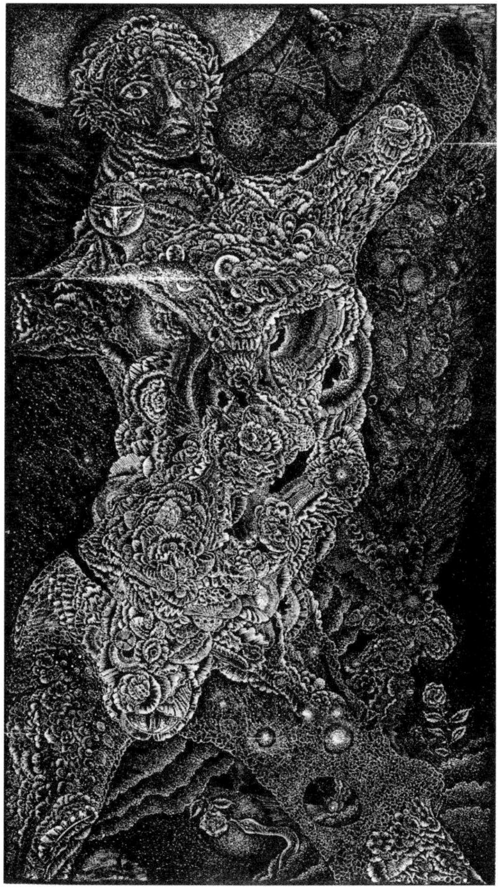

Hiwasaki *Rose in the Deeps*

from the block. It was in 1964, and he was a young man of twenty-three. From then on he began to work vigorously in the newly discovered medium, winning the gold prize at the Firenze Biennale in 1969 and many other prizes and awards.

Hiwasaki described his work as chiselling out light from darkness. Each stroke of a burin is to capture the light hidden in the depth of darkness, the inked surface of the block, dot by dot and line by line, gradually creating an image. This rather romantic concept of wood engraving inspired many younger artists, including Hitoshi Karasawa.

Karasawa was studying at Sokei School of Art, where he was taught by Hiwasaki who was there briefly as a visiting lecturer. Soon Karasawa himself started to teach at Sokei, producing at the same time an ambitious series of wood engravings. Among their pupils were Masahiro Kurita and Susumu Yamamoto, and in 1977 the four of them and Sho Kidokoro, who had also taught himself wood engraving, formed a group called 'Nomi no Kai' (society of chisels). Keisei Kobayashi joined them two years later. The society became the core of their prolific activities; they distinguished themselves by winning prestigious prizes both in Japan and abroad; many poets and writers were drawn to them in publishing and exhibiting together. This was the golden age of wood engraving in Japan. Kidokoro died in 1988 and Hiwasaki in 1992, both in their early fifties, but Karasawa, Kurita and Kobayashi are still very active and influential today.

There are younger generations of wood engravers, many of them inspired and influenced by Hiwasaki and Karasawa and the other members of 'Nomi no Kai' in one way or another. Their number is small – 15 to 20 full-scale wood engravers and a larger number of artists who try their hands at wood engraving as a way of printmaking while also engaged in copperplate or etching or woodcut.

Hiwasaki *Kalpa*

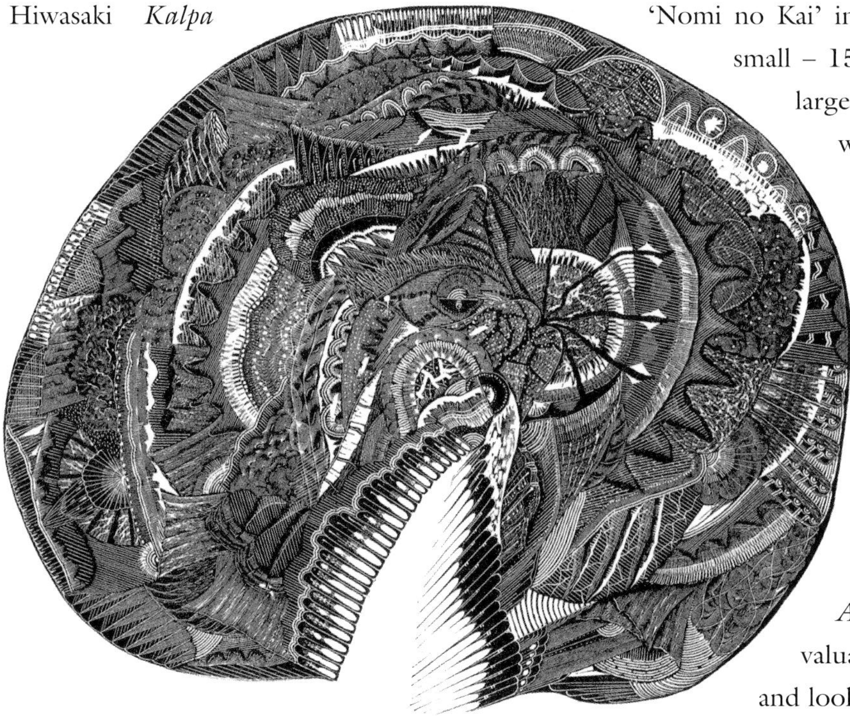

I have been engaged in promoting the work of some British wood engravers in Japan and had not personally known Japanese artists except one or two, until I was asked by Simon Brett to liaise with them with a view to persuading them to take part in his book project which became *An Engraver's Globe.* This has given me valuable opportunities to get to know them and look at their work with greater interest.

It is not easy to describe the characteristics of the work of Japanese artists in comparison with those of British artists, because they vary a great deal, even though they are such a small number. On the whole they seem to be interested in or obsessed with the inner world, the mental or philosophical side of things; their work is often serious and meditative, heavy with symbolic meaning. Landscape and townscape are but metaphors for their state of mind, rather than their observation or interpretation of nature. One famous artist told me once that engraving on hard wood for many hours is a lonely and painstaking act; such an introspective process is naturally suited for looking deep into the inside of human consciousness. In wood engraving, unlike in some other genres of art, spontaneity is restricted: every stroke of the tool has to be so carefully controlled that it is very natural for the artist to be withdrawn and introspective; or conversely an introspective type of person tends to choose wood engraving as a means of self-expression. Such an artist would be content with being isolated (or indeed enjoy it) and having no comradeship with other artists or the outside world; he will be happy enough with a small group of like-minded artists and people who understand and appreciate his work. His subject matter may be self-conscious, gloomy, and even draped with the shadow of death. It was difficult to persuade an artist of such a strong view to join the project: he was not in need of communication with other wood engravers, let alone those of other countries, for he is primarily interested in his own work and in himself, not interested whether the outside world understands him or not. It sounds as if he were a recluse; in fact he is well-established and regarded as the representative artist of this genre in Japan, having won many illustrious prizes and honours, and so he can assume an air of proud isolation and indifference to the recognition by the outside world. But I have found that he is not the only one; some others showed similar attitudes.

On the other hand there are some younger artists who are interested in other people's work or feedback on their work, and they would take part in exhibitions abroad. One of them won the special prize for the overseas division of the Society of Wood Engravers Exhibition a couple years ago with a very ambitious work. I asked another artist, who is developing a fairy-tale-like world of her own, why she regularly sends her work to the exhibition of the Society. She says it is because Britain is the country where wood engraving originated and developed, and where its tradition is part of culture. It is gratifying that her work should be seen by discerning artists, and by the audience which is familiar with the art; she would like them to know that wood engraving is being practised in Japan. She is pleased when her work is purchased: that a total stranger likes her work well enough to pick it out is a simple but ultimate sign of appreciation of the work itself. It gives her a special

Rie Kawauchi
The Promise
Catalogue no. 41.

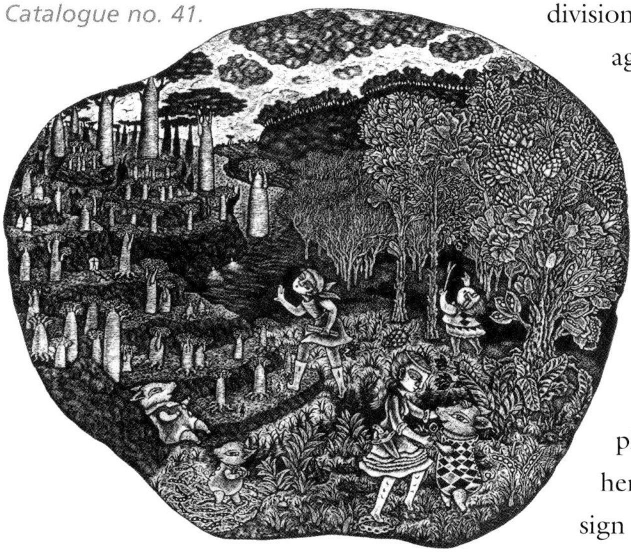

pleasure when she gets direct response to her work: one woman wrote to her saying that she had liked her work so much that she had chosen it as a present for her son, and asking about the possible story behind it.

This artist started oil painting at a very young age, influenced by her grandfather who was an artist, and was active enough to give five or six solo shows in her twenties. When she discovered wood engraving at the age of thirty, however, its impact was so strong that it changed her career: the contrast with oil painting was so refreshing and she saw rich possibility in the seemingly restricted scope of black and white. For twenty years since then, she has devoted herself to wood engraving. She briefly played with hand colouring but has reverted to black and white, in which she finds more room for imagination. She feels that she has now found the metier which suits her best.

Another woman artist works mainly in rich colours, using a complex method. Peonies and roses in red and pink or shimmering silver loom out of deep darkness. The piece may not look like wood engraving, but it is the finest black lines that define and enliven delicate petals, and the lines, sharp but characteristically warm, are nothing but those of wood engraving. She has taken courses in oil painting and copperplate but no formal training in wood engraving; this method is a fruit of many years of experiment. Unfortunately her work is not represented in *An Engraver's Globe*, since I came to know it only after the editing of the book was completed. I hope she will agree to send her work to the Society's exhibition in the near future.

Most of the Japanese artists I have met seem to have a group of collectors, some of whom are quite faithful. In the case of the famous artist I spoke of above, some collectors are keen enough to order a set of twelve or fifteen prints from the catalogue by calling the gallery on the first day of a show. This niche market is like a secret society, in which members prefer it to be closed: the more exclusive the better. Direct contact with the artist himself is an added bonus. The working of this market is a mystery to an outsider like me.

ALIS (Arts & Literature International Service), which I started eleven years ago, is a small private company promoting British wood engraving in Japan, and is still the only one of its kind to my knowledge. The market for British wood engraving, which was almost nil when we started, is still very small and limited, but I like to think that it is growing gradually. Roughly speaking, it consists of two groups: a small number of professional people including artists, museum curators and academics would go for technical perfection and conceptual interest, while the other larger group of general audience tend to be attracted to representation of life in Britain: landscapes, village scenes, gardens and flowers, and cats, as well as literary themes. In spite of the disadvantage of not having the artists' presence, and the serious economic depression, as well as our own limited resources, our annual exhibition of British wood engraving is doing quite well, attracting a larger and a wider variety of audience. I sincerely hope that more British artists will agree to participate in it in the future.

THE 66TH ANNUAL EXHIBITION 2003–2004

This exhibition is drawn from an open submission. All forms of relief print are eligible and all work, whether by members or non-members, is selected by a committee which changes each year. This year, the selection committee was chaired by Hilary Paynter with Kate Dicker and Jim Westergard.

Prices are for UNFRAMED PRINTS. Unframed prints may be ordered by post and will normally arrive within two weeks but longer if they are coming from overseas. Please let us know if an order is urgent. In most cases, there are plenty available. However, occasionally an edition sells out.

Prices for framed prints are available on application, but the framed print can only be collected at the end of the tour.

THE RACHEL RECKITT PRIZES

Rachel Reckitt first exhibited with the Society of Wood Engravers in 1933 while a student of Iain Macnab's at the Grosvenor School of Modern Art; she continued to exhibit regularly up until the 1993–4 tour. Following her death in 1995 the bulk of her estate went to set up a grant-giving charitable trust, The Golsoncott Foundation, whose declared aim is *to promote, maintain, improve and advance the education of the public in the arts generally and in particular the fine arts and music.* The fostering of the practice and appreciation of the arts, especially amongst young people and new audiences, is a further specific objective.

The trustees wished to continue Rachel's encouragement of wood engraving and have established two annual prizes for British or

Commonwealth engravers, each of £500; one would be an open prize and the other restricted to engravers of 35 and under. The prizes will be awarded for ten years and then reviewed. The winners are chosen by the selection committee of the SWE. At the end of the annual tour the prize-winning prints will be donated to a museum or other institution to be decided by the Trustees. The foundation encourages applications that meet its aims as set out above; guidelines may be obtained from The Administrator, The Golsoncott Foundation, 31 Danes Road, Exeter EX4 4LS.

2003 PRIZE WINNERS

The Rachel Reckitt Open Prize:
Peter Lawrence *Isola Bella, Lake Maggiore* *Catalogue no. 52.*

The Rachel Reckitt Open Prize for a wood engraver under 35 years of age:
Alex Smart *The Cottage – Charlton* *Catalogue no. 94.*

The SWE prizes for outstanding engravings from overseas:
Peter Lazarov *Shoji 3* *Catalogue no. 54.*
Richard Wagener *Tundra* *Catalogue no. 110.*

LIST OF MEMBERS

HONORARY MEMBERS

Diana Bloomfield
James Bostock
Anatoli Kalashnikov
Frank Martin
John O'Connor

Editor of Multiples
Sheila Hönigsberg

MEMBERS

Rosalind Atkins
Rosalind Bliss
Peter Bosteels
G Brender à Brandis
Simon Brett
John Bryce
Harry Brockway
Claire Dalby
Chris Daunt
Andrew Davidson
Furio de Denaro
Anne Desmet
Kate Dicker
Anthony Dunigan
E N Ellis
Andy English
Jonathan Gibbs
Raymond Gloeckler
David Hackman
Anne Hayward
Clare Hemstock
Linda Holmes
John Howson
H J Jackson
Pauline Jacobsen
Patricia Jaffé
Judith Jaidinger
Cordelia Jones
Anne Jope
Paul L Kershaw
Rosemary Kilbourn
Beth Krommes
John Lawrence
Peter Lawrence
Peter Lazarov
Kathleen Lindsley
Jane Lydbury
Miriam Macgregor
Vitaly Moiseev
John Morley
Ian Mortimer
M J Mott
David Moyer
Hilary Paynter
Pam Pebworth
Howard Phipps
Julian Poole
Arkady Pugachevsky
Gennady Pugachevsky
Peter Reddick
Abigail Rorer
Ronald Salmond
Ben Sands
Sue Scullard
Colin See-Paynton
Derek Setford
Pauline Sitwell
Yvonne Skargon
Campbell Smith
Shirley Smith
Edward Stamp
Ian Stephens
Sybella Stiles
Eva Stockhaus
James Todd
Ann Tout
George Tute
Jeroen van Duyn
Sarah van Niekerk
Geri Waddington
Richard Wagener
Jim Westergard
Graham Williams
Chris Wormell

COMMITTEE

Chairman
Hilary Paynter
Honorary Secretary
Ann Tout
Honorary Treasurer
Nigel Hamway

Harry Brockway
Kate Dicker
Peter Lawrence
Jane Lydbury

Sales Secretary
Julian Johnston

1
Paula Allerton
A/P III
MDF / LINO
£100

2
Marcus Beaven
Hogweed
WOOD ENGRAVING
£38

3
Rachel Beckett
Over the Green
WOOD ENGRAVING
£20

4
Marina Bindella
Arcaica I
PVC ENGRAVING
£250

5
Hubert Borys
The Oval
LINOCUT
£250

6
Simon Brett
In Which God May Dwell
WOOD ENGRAVING
£160

7
Simon Brett
Run for your Country,
Run for your Life
WOOD ENGRAVING
£175

8
Simon Brett
Disunion Jacks
WOOD ENGRAVING
£175

9
Harry Brockway
Frankenstein on the Ice
WOOD ENGRAVING
£60

10
Harry Brockway
Frankenstein and the Monster
WOOD ENGRAVING
£60

11
Harry Brockway
Harvesting Kelp
WOOD ENGRAVING
£50

12
John Bryce
Roofs and Doorways
WOOD ENGRAVING
£110

13
John Bryce
Brentford Boatyard
WOOD ENGRAVING
£70

14
Anne Cathcart
Nouns of Assemblage 2
A Zig Zag of Zebras
WOOD ENGRAVING
£50

15
Sally Cole
Cormorant
WOOD ENGRAVING
£25

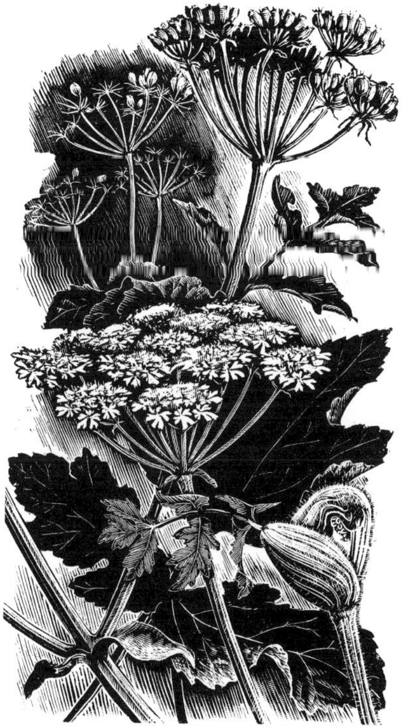

2

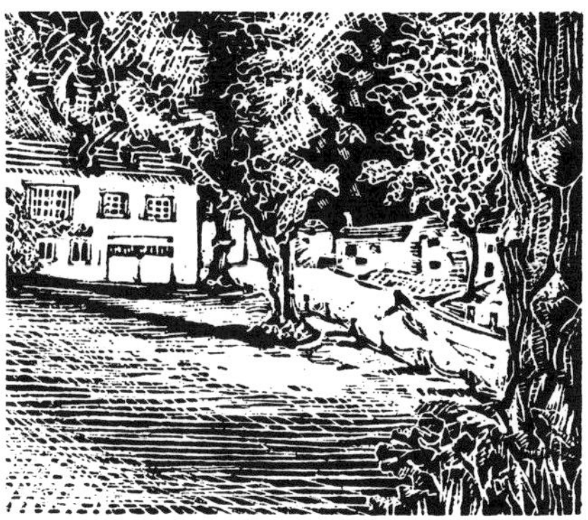

3

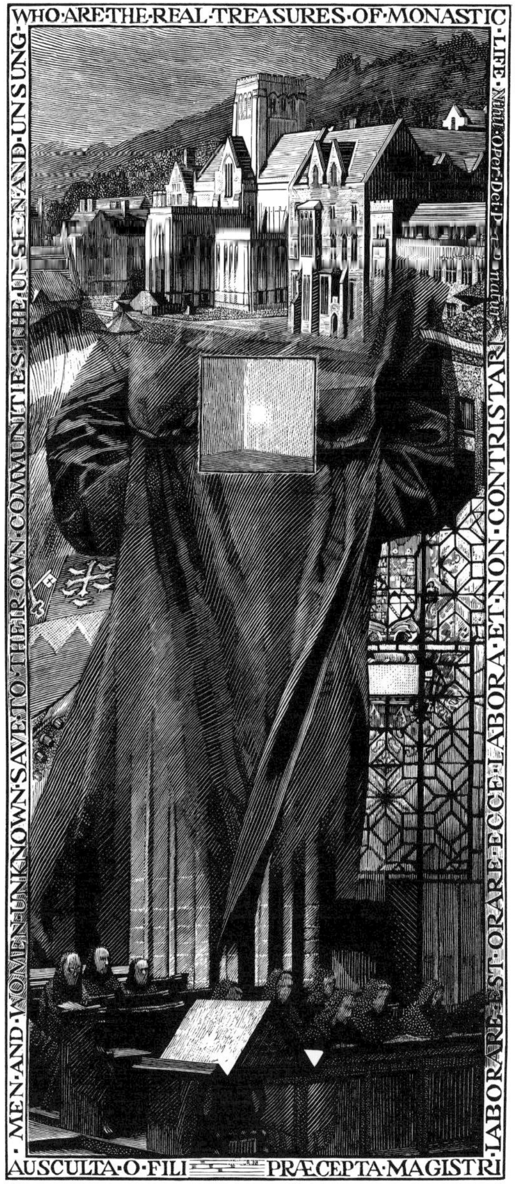
WHO·ARE·THE·REAL·TREASURES·OF·MONASTIC
LIFE·Nihil·Operi·Dei·P
·MEN·AND·WOMEN·UNKNOWN·SAVE·TO·THEIR·OWN·COMMUNITIES·THE·UNSEEN·AND·UNSUNG·
LABORARE·EST·ORARE·ECCE·LABORA·ET·NON·CONTRISTARI
AUSCULTA·O·FILI
PRÆCEPTA·MAGISTRI

6

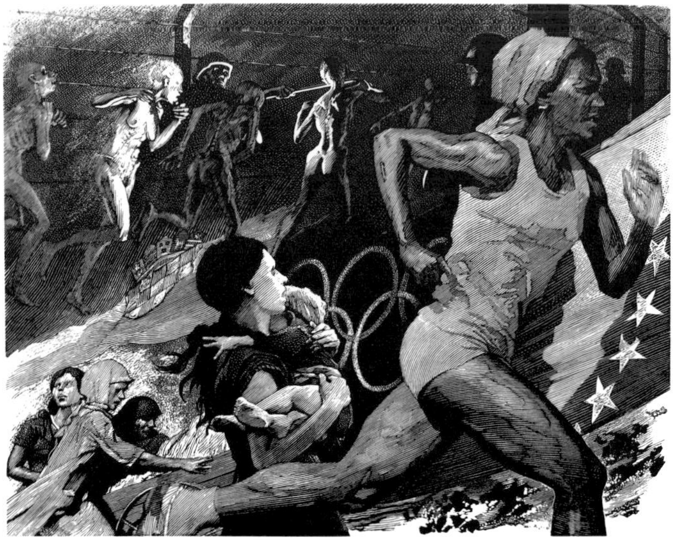

7

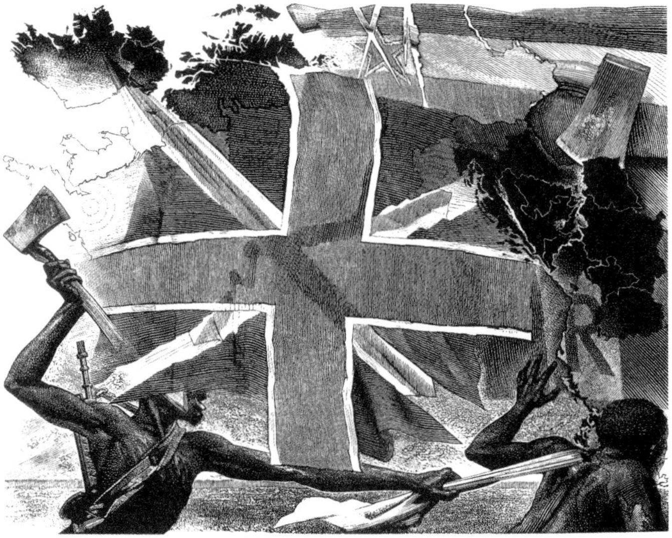

8

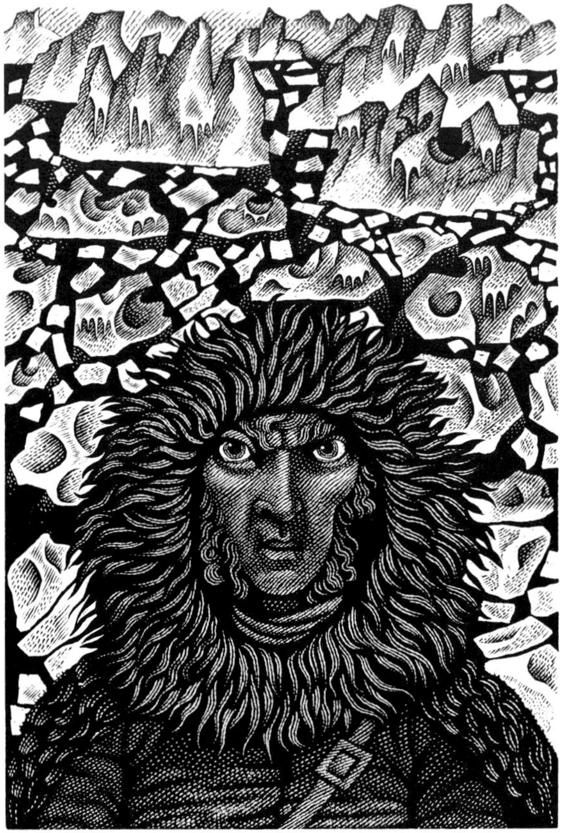

9

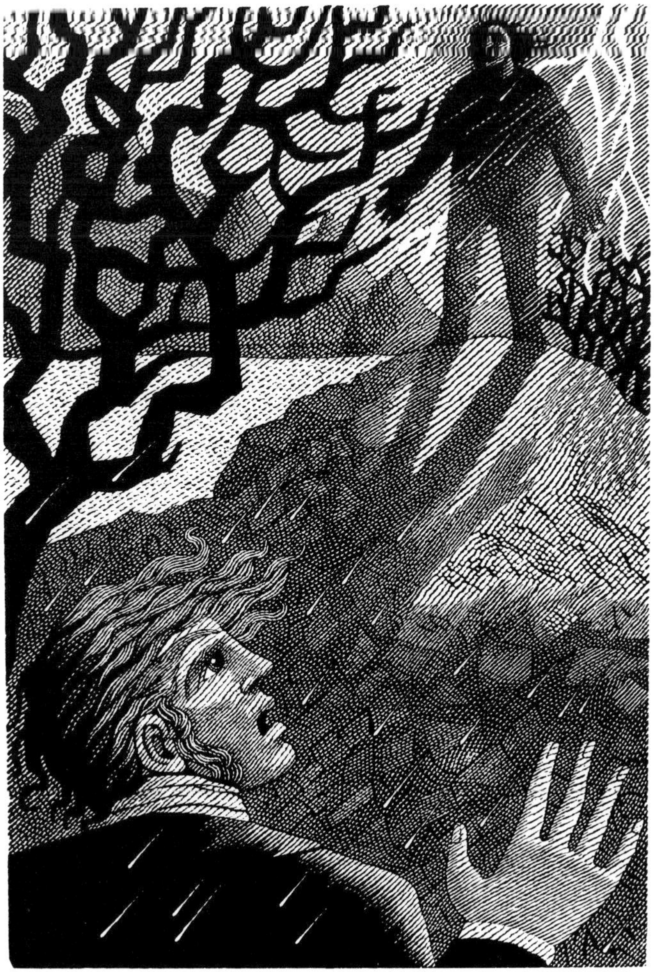

10

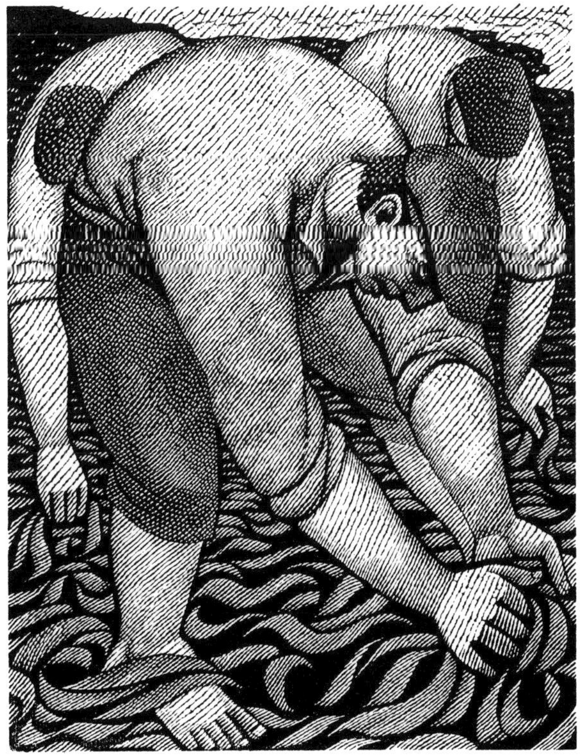

11

12

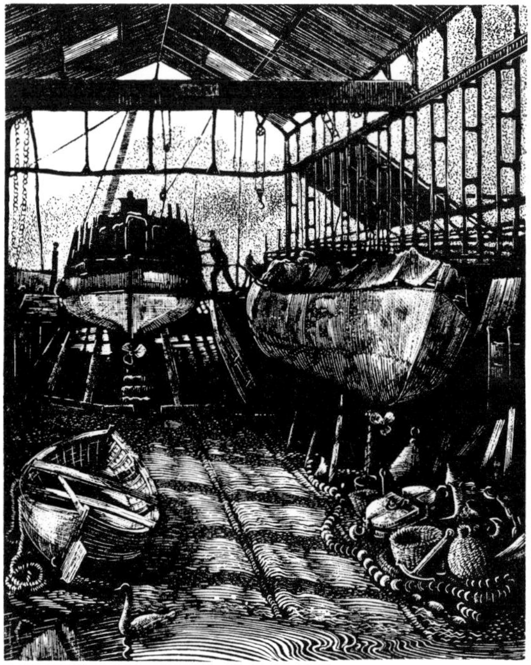

13

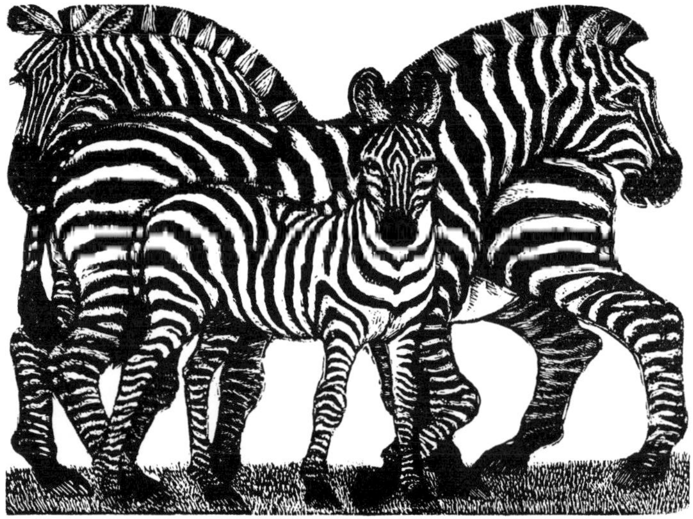

14

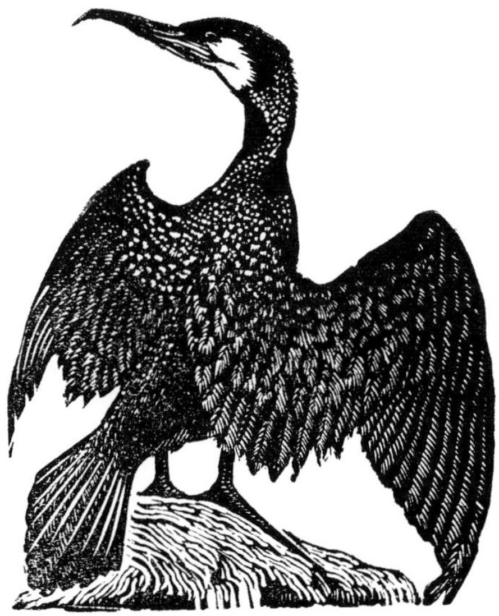

15

16
A J Cundall
Profilia
WOOD ENGRAVING
£50

17
Claire Dalby
Rhubarb Pots
WOOD ENGRAVING
£65

18
Chris Daunt
The Organist
WOOD ENGRAVING
£56

19
Chris Daunt
Margery Kempe
WOOD ENGRAVING
£42

20
Daniel Dennison
Priest's Cove, Series 3
WOOD ENGRAVING
£90

21 *see page 39*
Anne Desmet
Thirty Pieces of Wood
MIXED MEDIA
£950 framed

22 *see page 39*
Anne Desmet
Teatro Romano
LINOCUT
£570

23 *see page 39*
Anne Desmet
Kremlin Christmas
MIXED MEDIA
£700 framed

24
Kate Dicker
"Float it"
WOOD ENGRAVING
£45

25
Kate Dicker
Peace March
WOOD ENGRAVING
£45

26
Anthony Dunigan
Herringfleet Mill
PLASTIC ENGRAVING
£90

27
Andy English
Pam's Desk
In Memoriam – Pamela Hughes
WOOD ENGRAVING
£32

28
Richard M Franklin
Variation I
MIXED MEDIA
£82

29 *see page 40*
Richard M Franklin
Variation II
MIXED MEDIA
£82

30
Raymond Gloeckler
King Fisher's Tale
WOOD ENGRAVING
£100

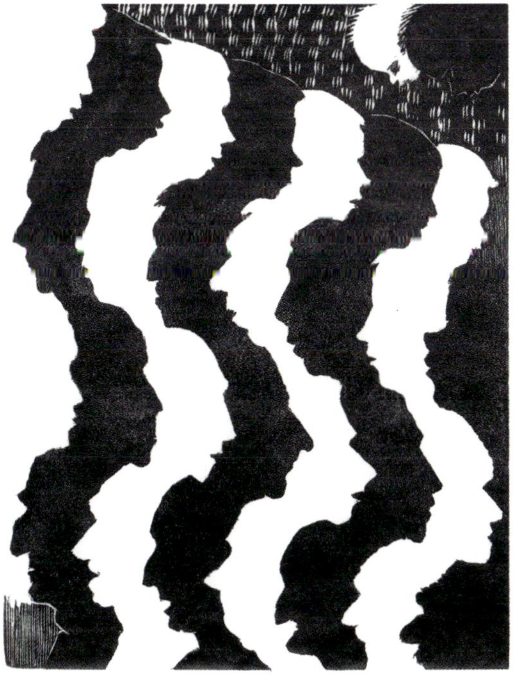

16

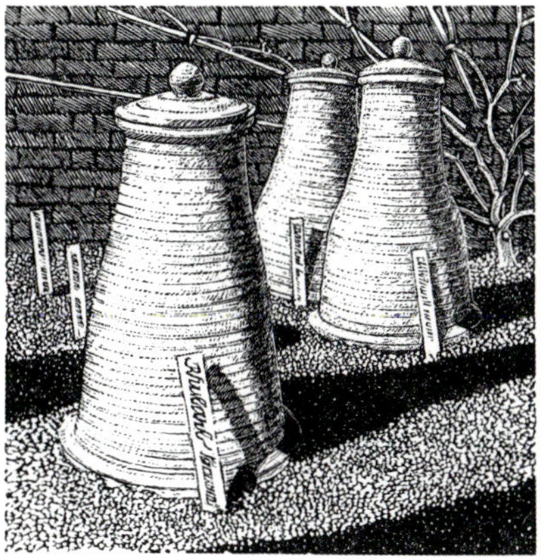

17

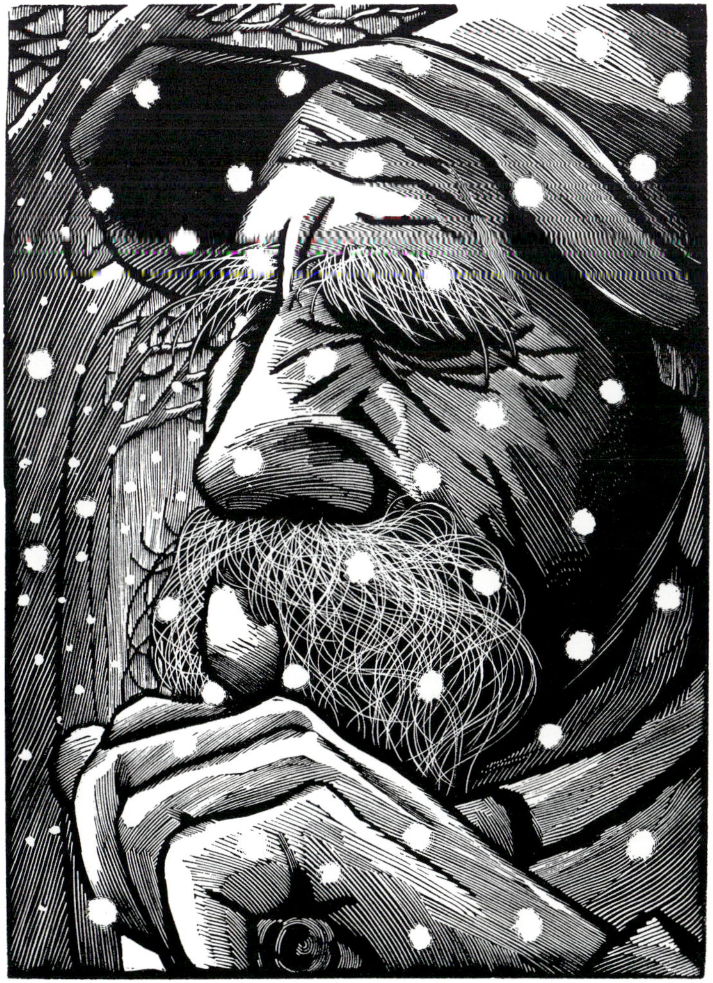

18

from The Society's 2001 publication,
A Polish Christmas by Maria Dabrowska

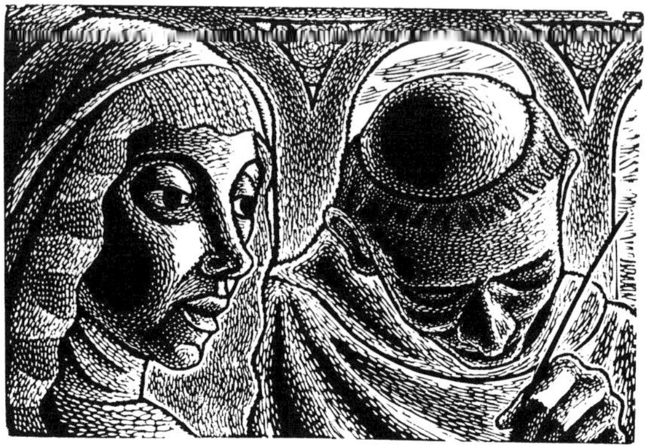

19

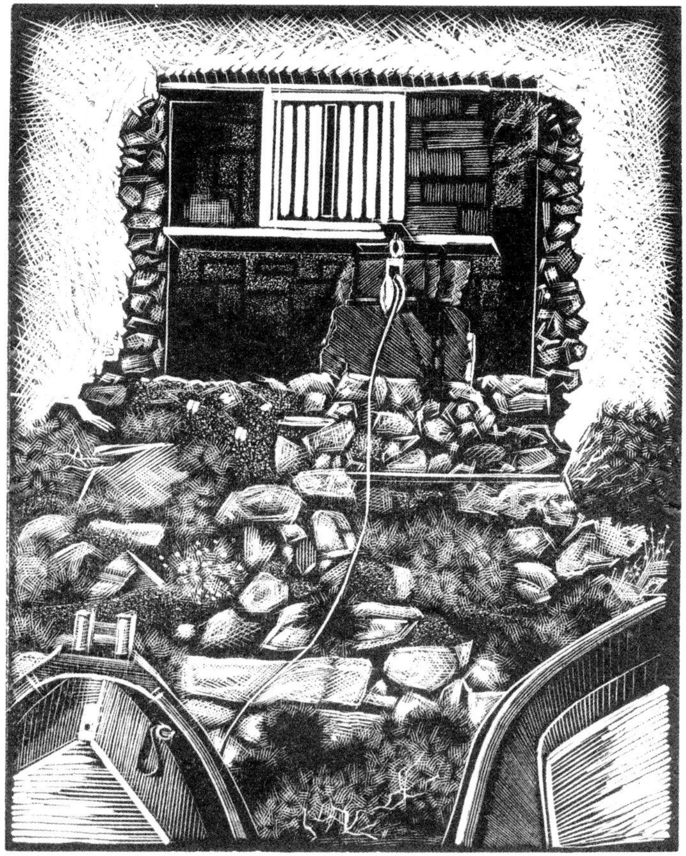

20

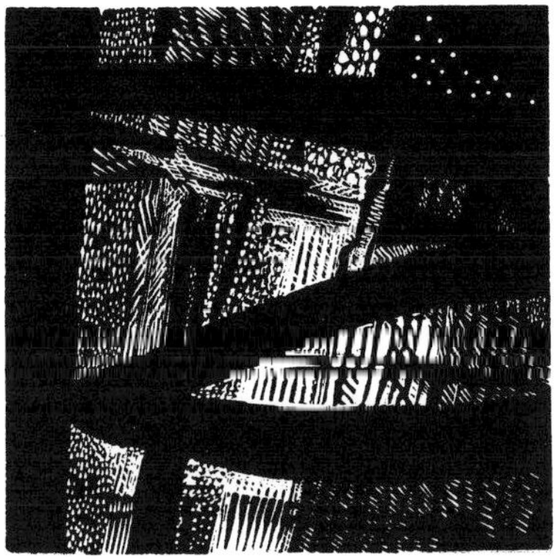
24

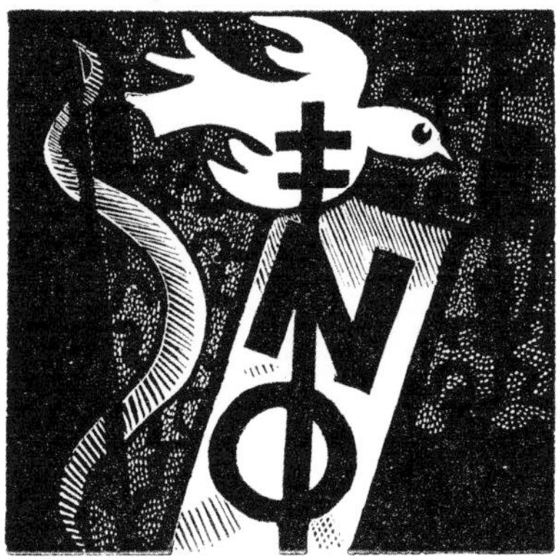
25

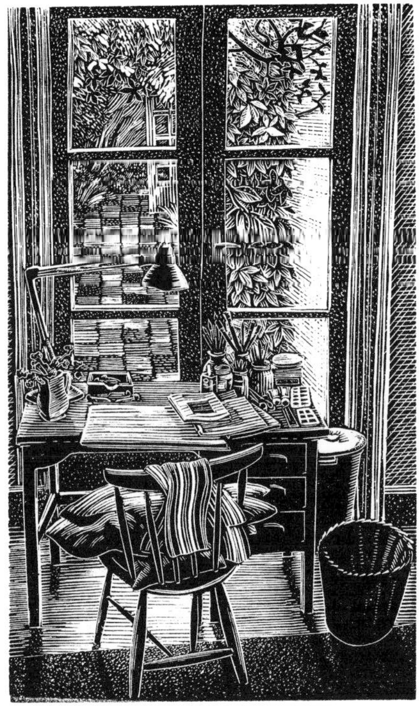
27

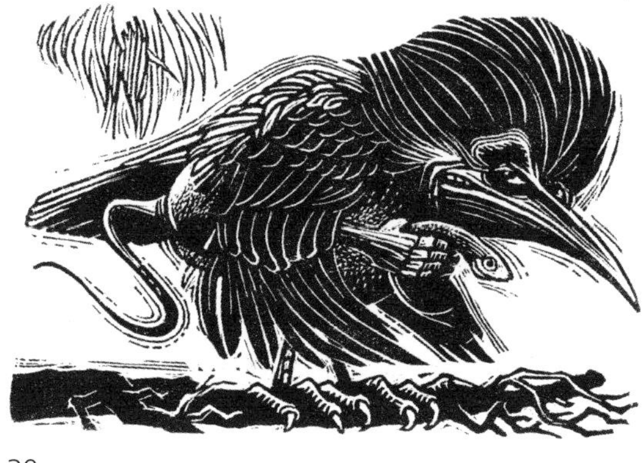
30

31
Raymond Gloeckler
The Ognar Fish
WOOD ENGRAVING
£95

32
David Hackman
The Pear Tree
WOOD ENGRAVING
£85

33
David Hackman
Shadows & Cracked Paving
WOOD ENGRAVING
£60

34
David Hackman
Winchelsea Breakwater
WOOD ENGRAVING
£85

35
Trevor Haddrell
Seat on Brandon Hill Bristol
VINYL ENGRAVING
£45

36
Ann Hayward
September Morning
WOOD ENGRAVING
£35

37
Ann Hayward
The Ides of March
WOOD ENGRAVING
£35

38
H J Jackson
Boats and Tractors
LINOCUT
£155

39
Pauline Jacobsen
Isaiah 43
WOODCUT
£120

40
Judy Jaidinger
Oh Future, Thou Secreted Place
WOOD ENGRAVING
£140

41 *see page 20*
Rie Kawauchi
The Promise
WOOD ENGRAVING
£215

42
Rie Kawauchi
The Encampment
WOOD ENGRAVING
£200

43
Gillian Kenny
Baobab Tree
WOOD ENGRAVING
£50

44
Paul L Kershaw
From End to End
WOOD ENGRAVING
£100

45
Paul L Kershaw
Outside In
WOOD ENGRAVING
£50

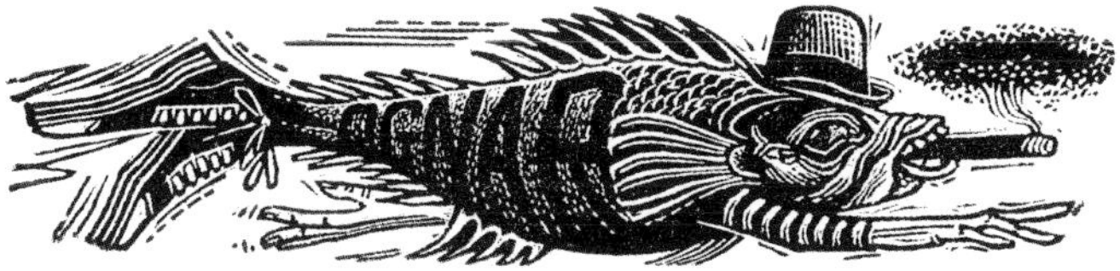

31

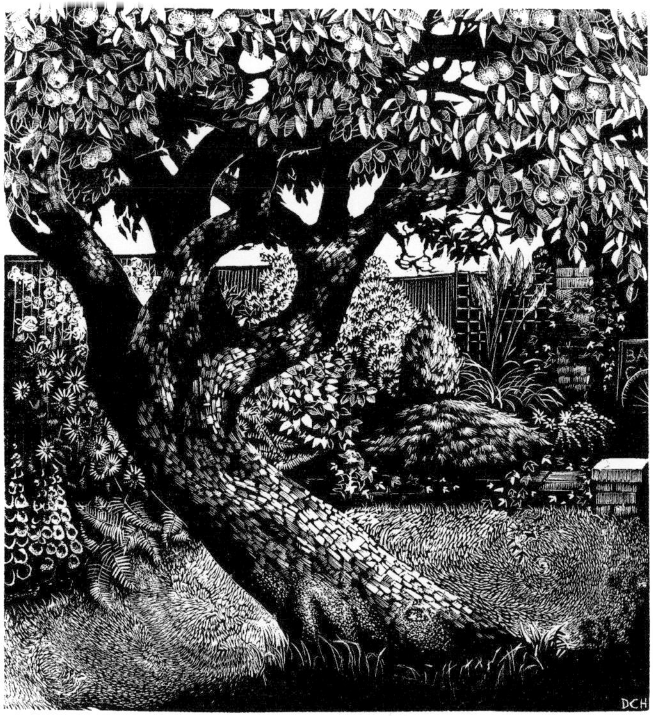

32

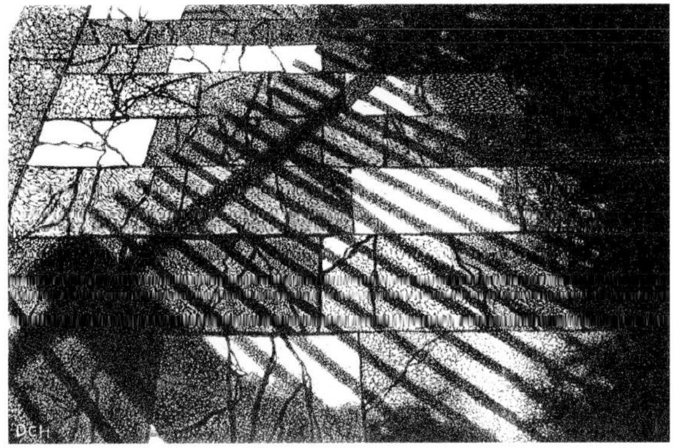

33

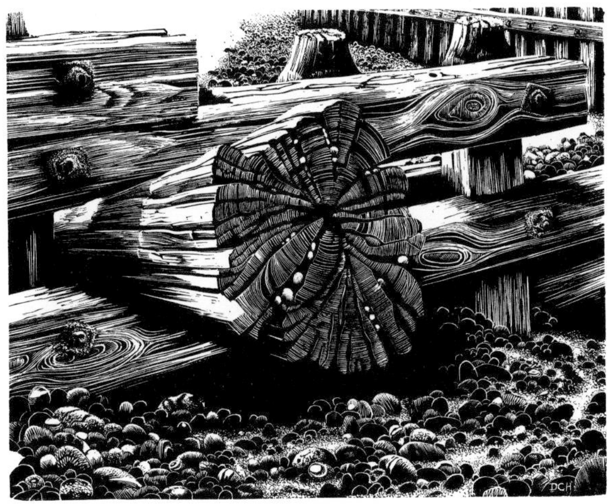

34

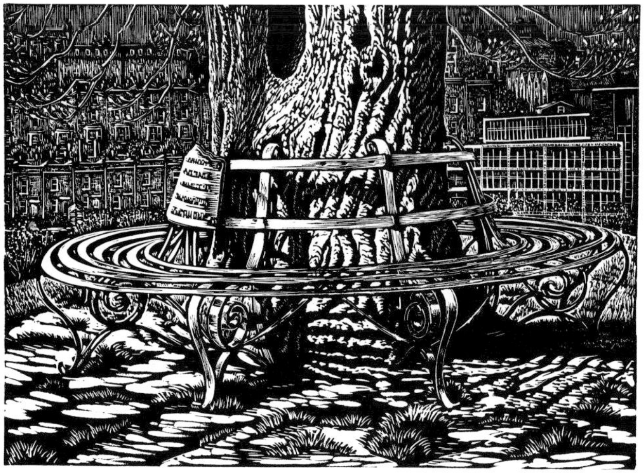

35

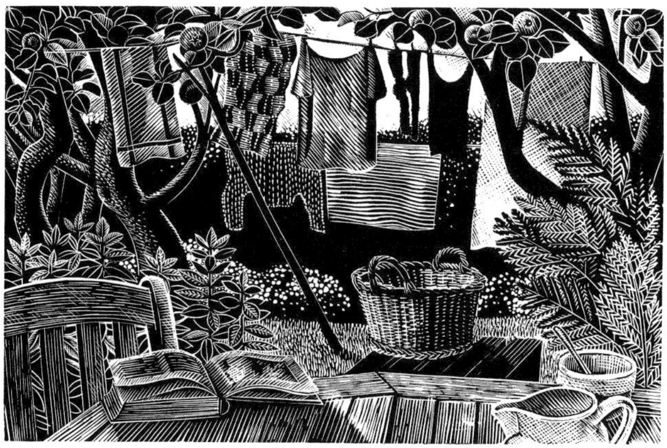

36

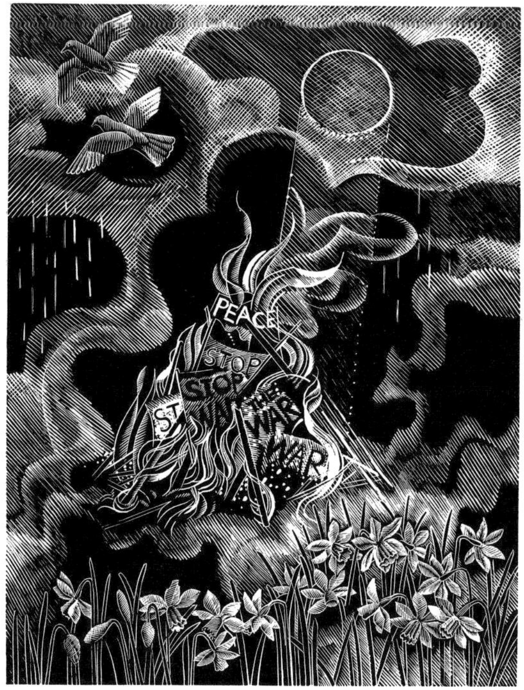

37

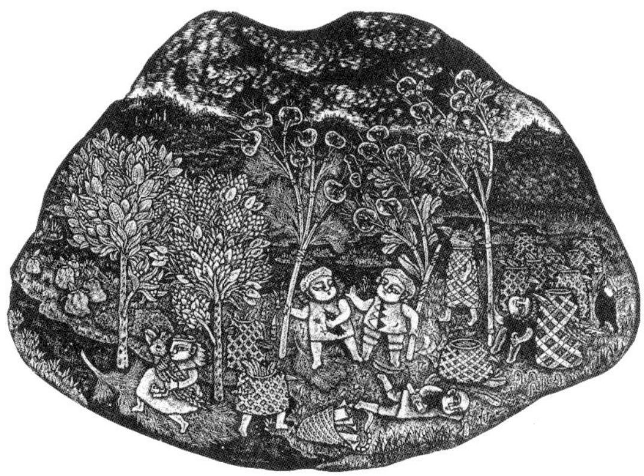

42

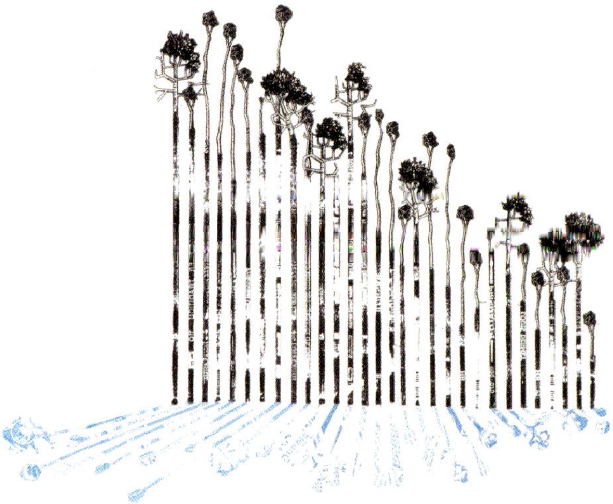

21

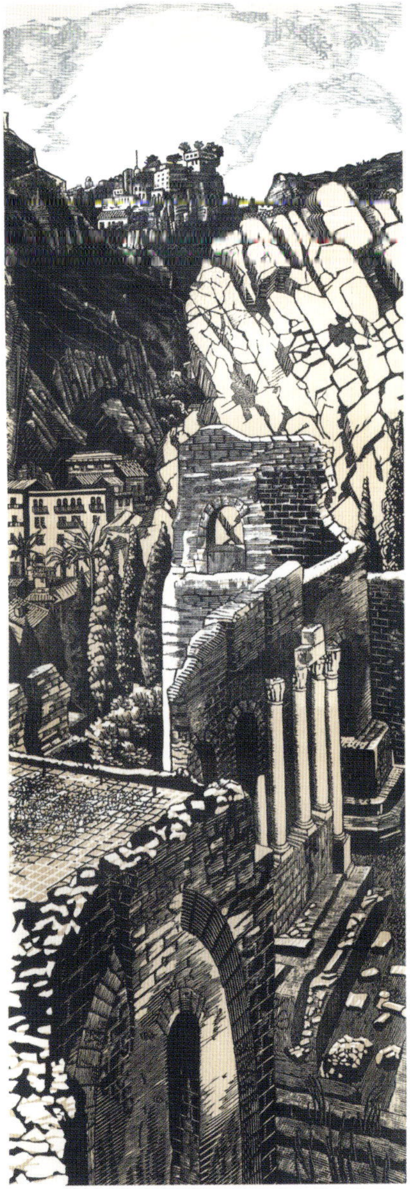

22

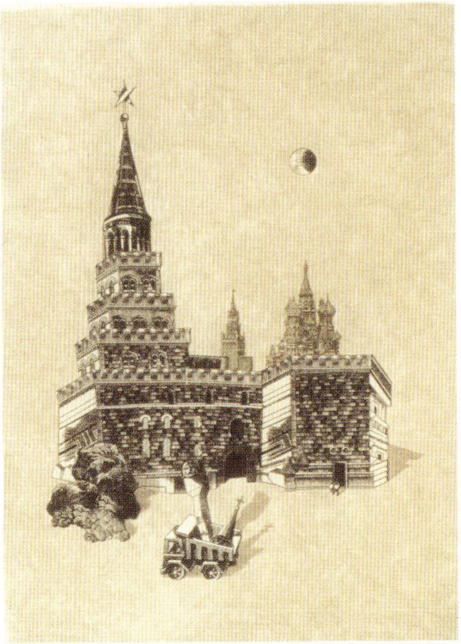

23

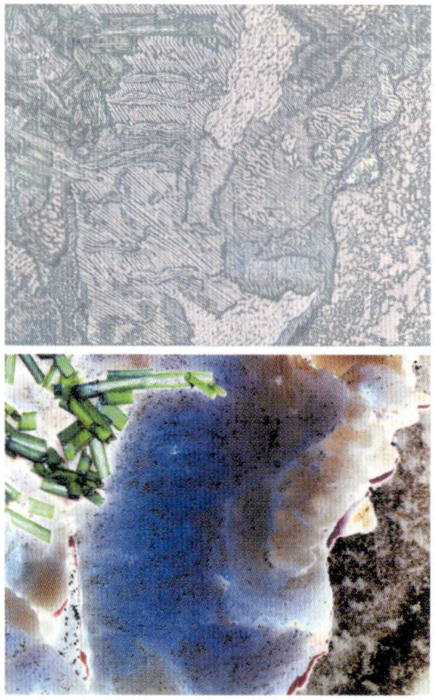

29

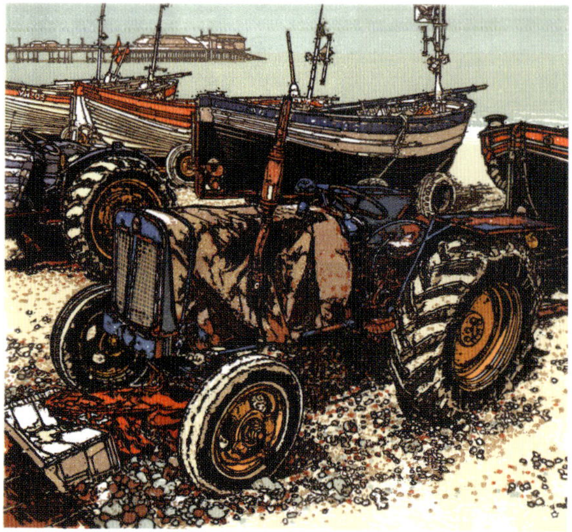

38

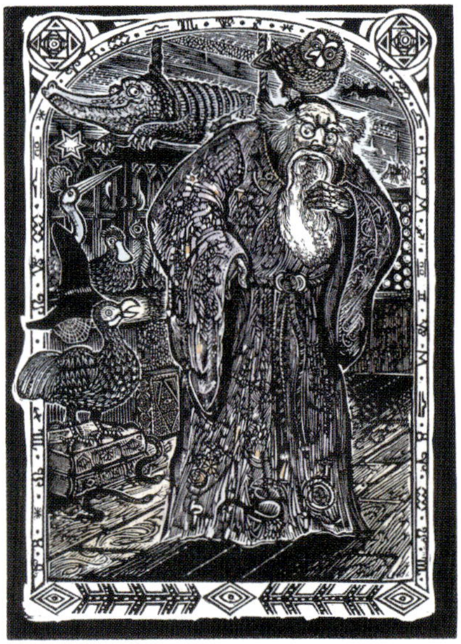

49

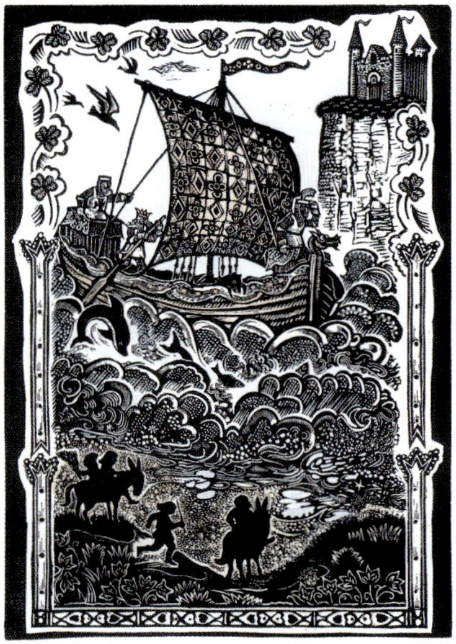

50

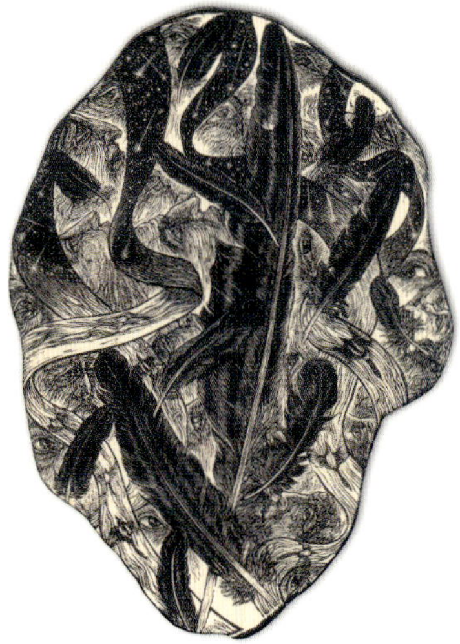

63

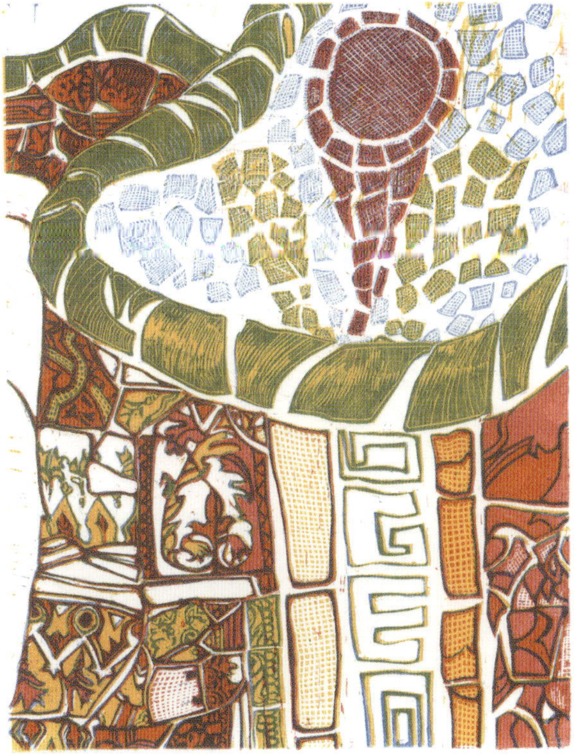
69

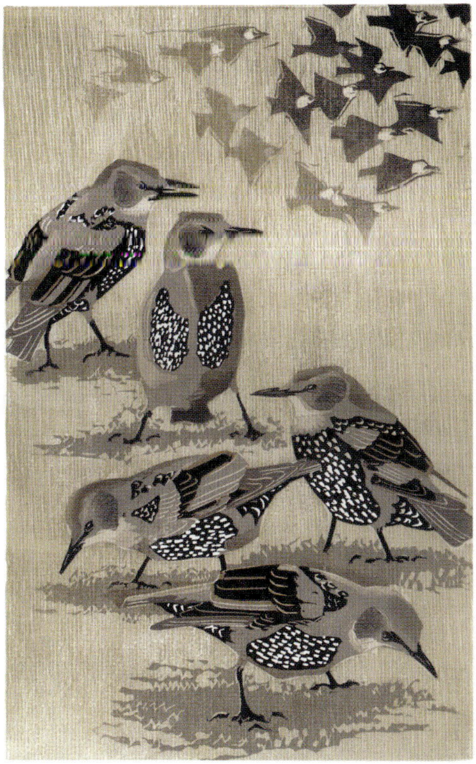
97

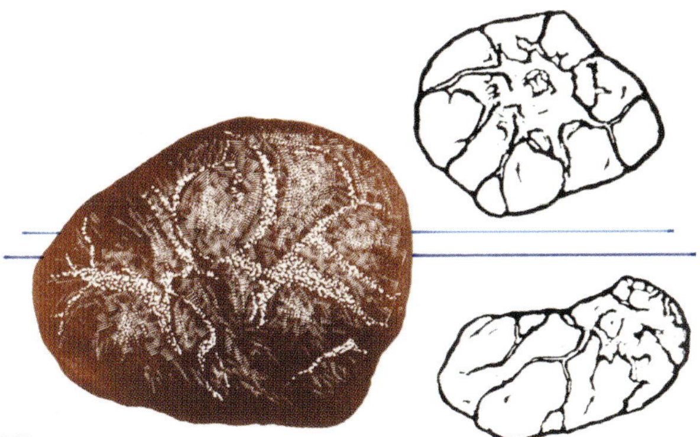
70

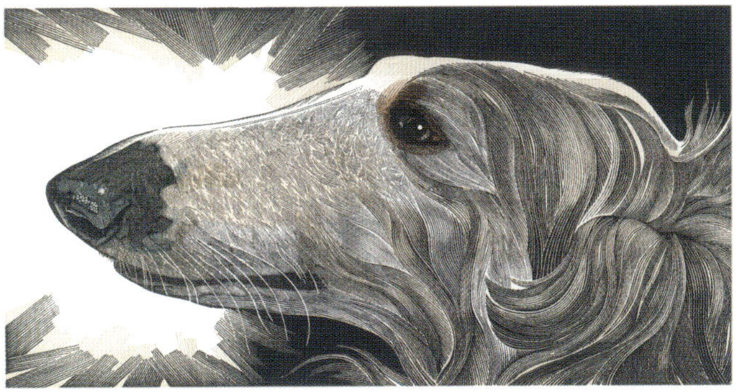
82

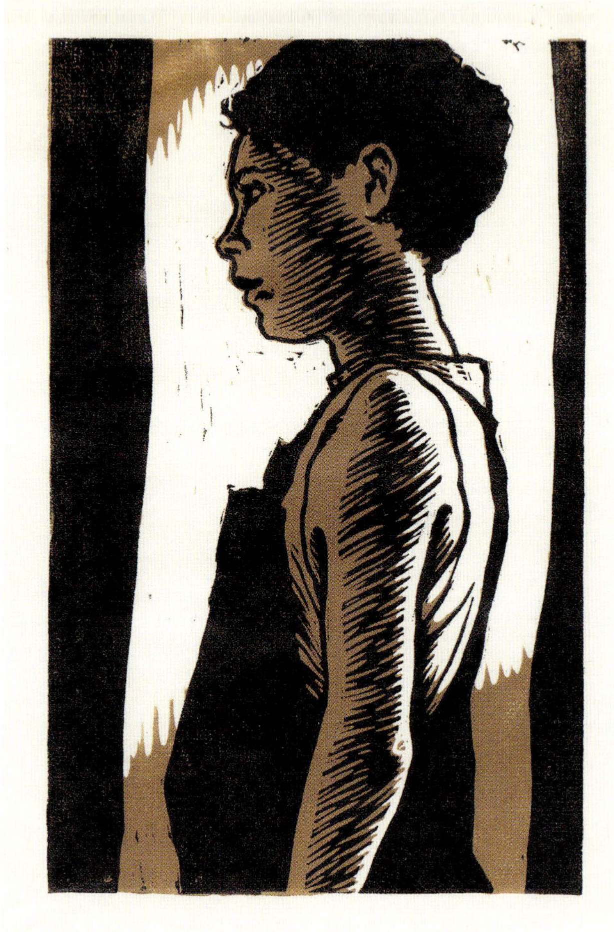

114

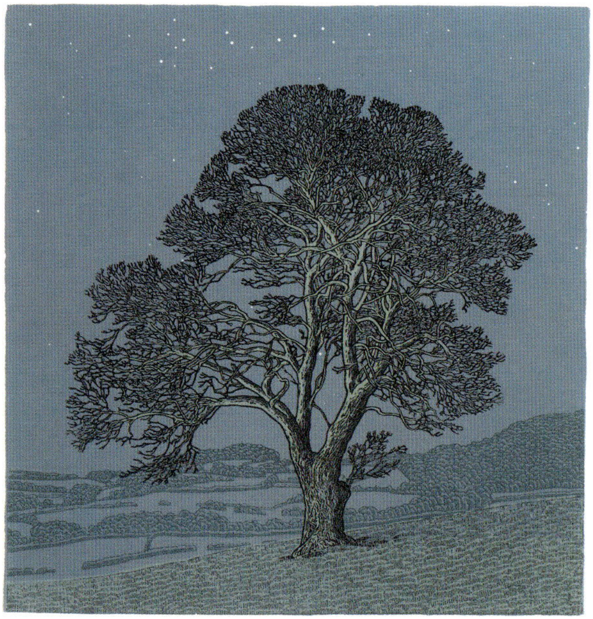

106

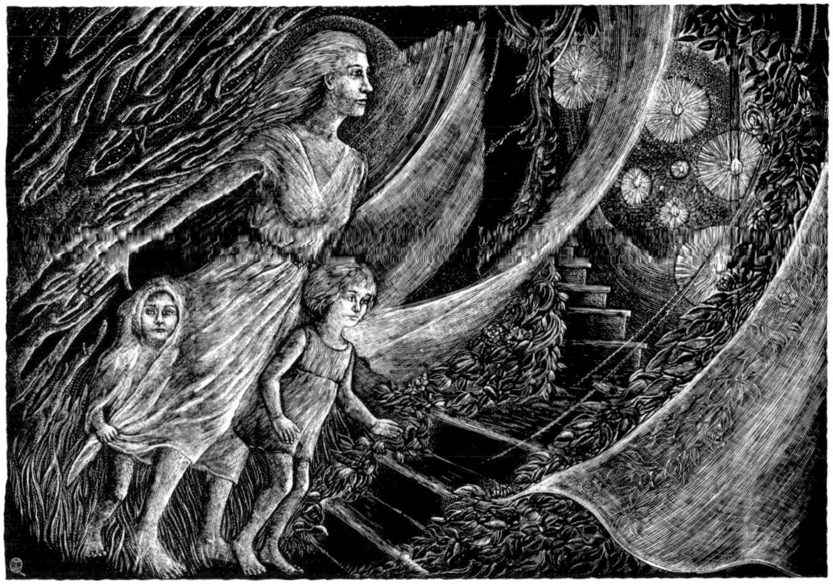

40

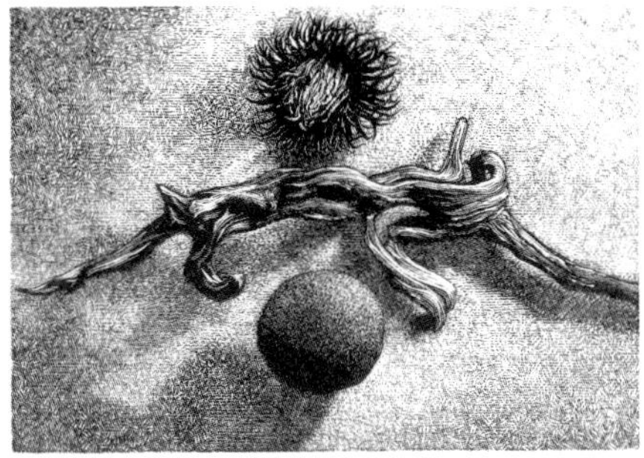

45

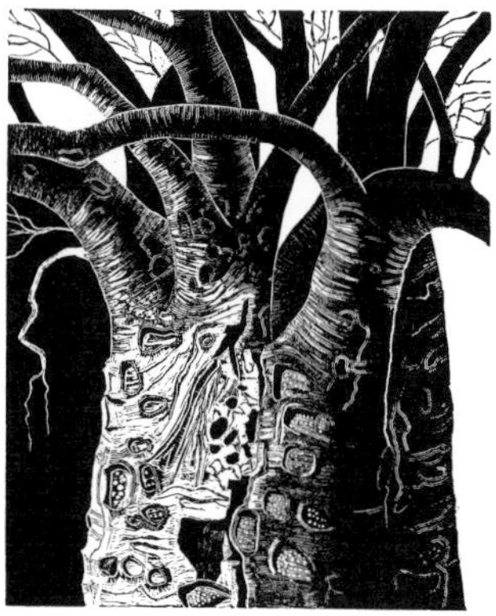

43

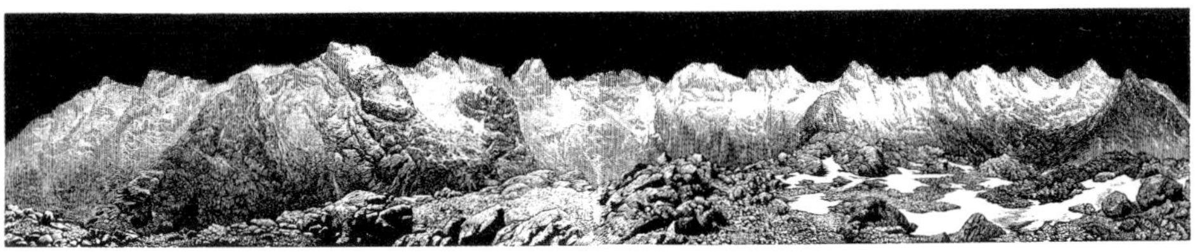

44

46
Paul L Kershaw
Growing Still
WOOD ENGRAVING
£60

47
Rosemary Kilbourn
Pentecost
WOOD ENGRAVING
£250

48
Celina Kirchner
Untitled 57
LINOCUT
£120

49 *see page 40*
John Lawrence
*Merlin**
VINYL
£120

50 *see page 40*
John Lawrence
The Magic Barge
VINYL
£120

51
Peter Lawrence
Creative Review
RESINGRAVE
£150

52 *see cover*
Peter Lawrence
Isola Bella, Lake Maggiore
RESINGRAVE
£125

53
Peter Lawrence
Godrevy Island from the Hotel, St. Ives
RESINGRAVE
£60

54
Peter Lazarov
Shoji 3
WOOD ENGRAVING
£160

55
Peter Lazarov
Shoji 4
WOOD ENGRAVING
£160

56
Kathleen Lindsley
Hamara River, Glendale
WOOD ENGRAVING
£56

57
Kathleen Lindsley
Skye Shepherd 2000
WOOD ENGRAVING
£63

58
Kathleen Lindsley
Autumn Dawn, Colbost
WOOD ENGRAVING
£63

59
Susan Lowdermilk
State of Grace
RESINGRAVE
£110

60
Jane Lydbury
Untitled
WOOD ENGRAVING
£90

* from *The Once and Future King* The Folio Society 2003

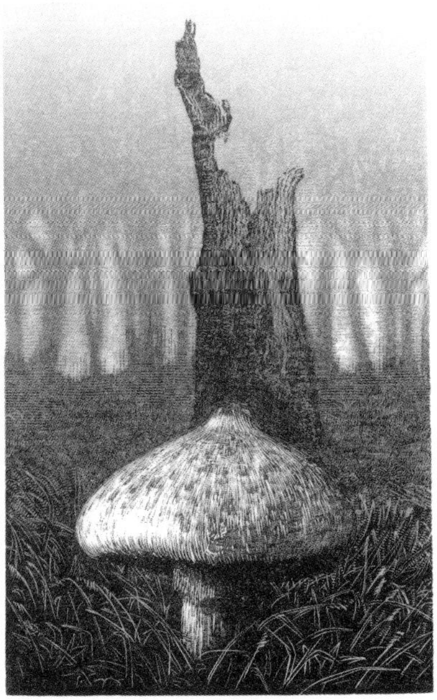

46

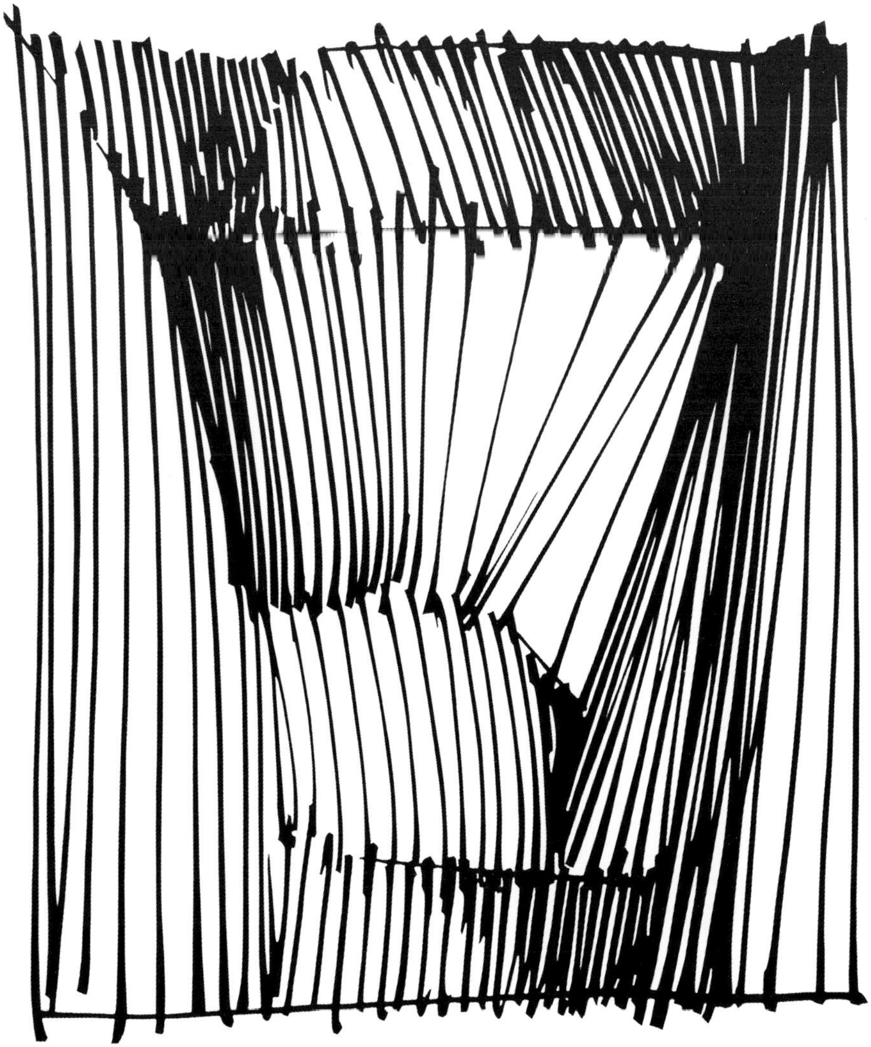

48

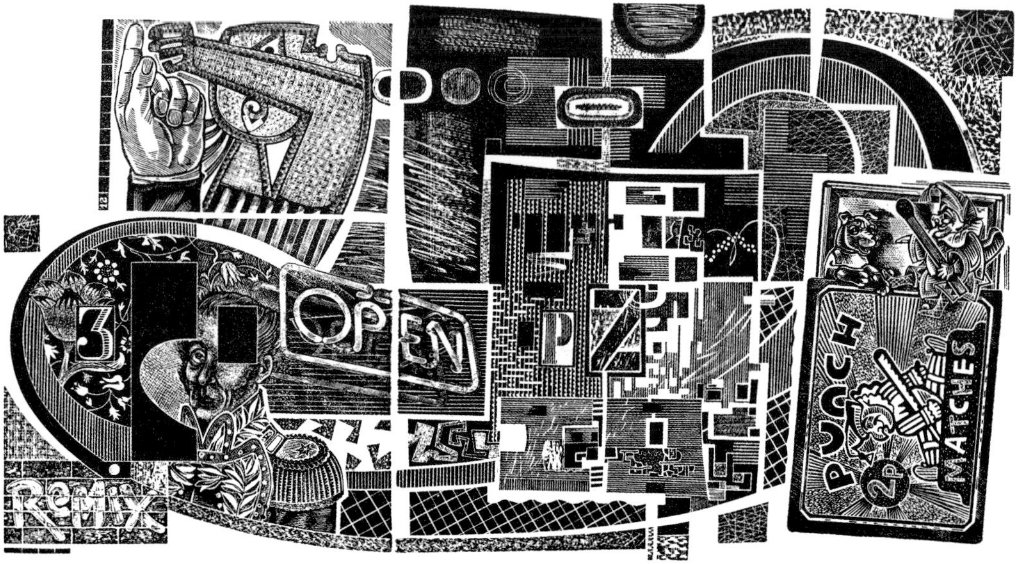

51

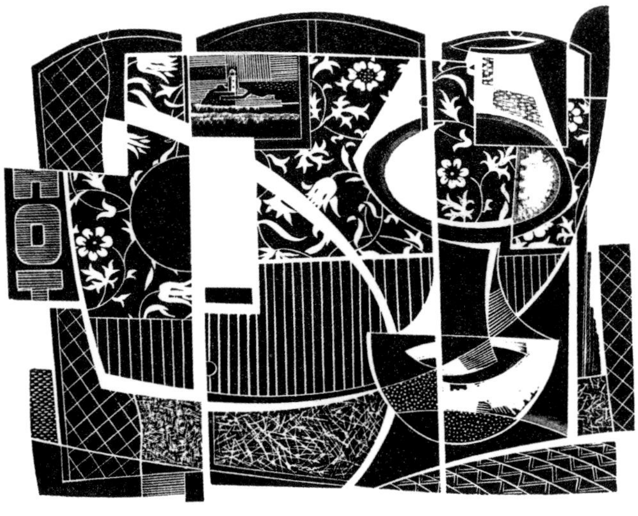

53

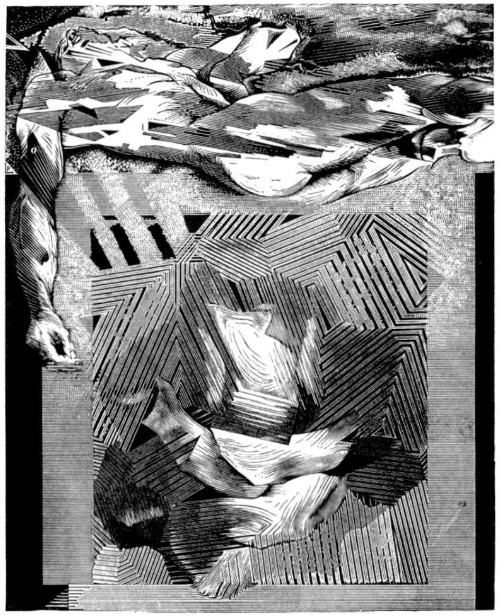

54

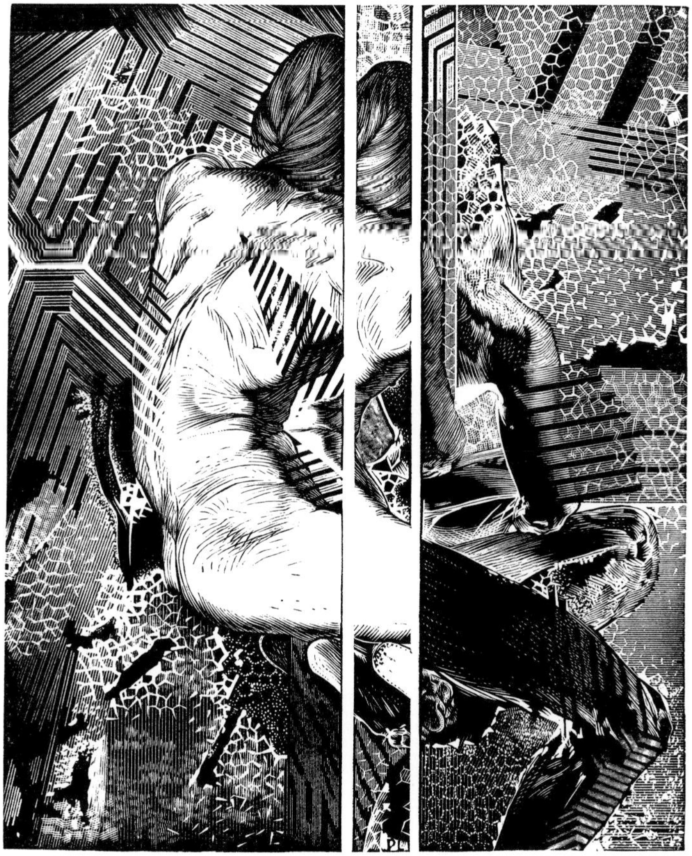

55

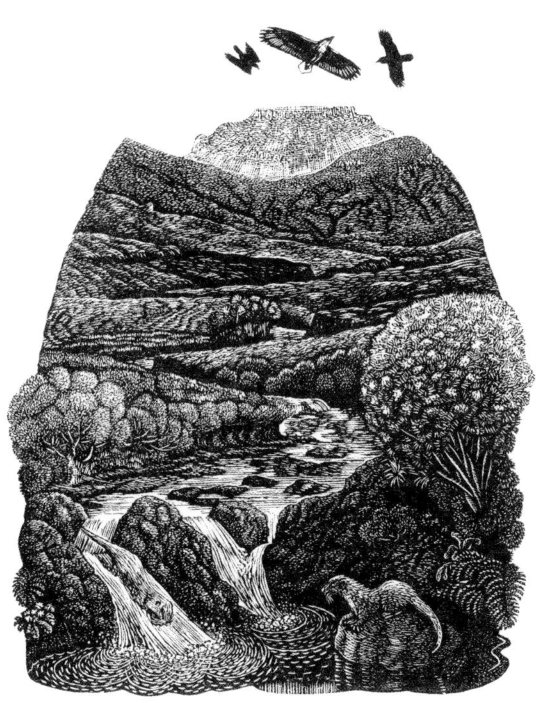

56

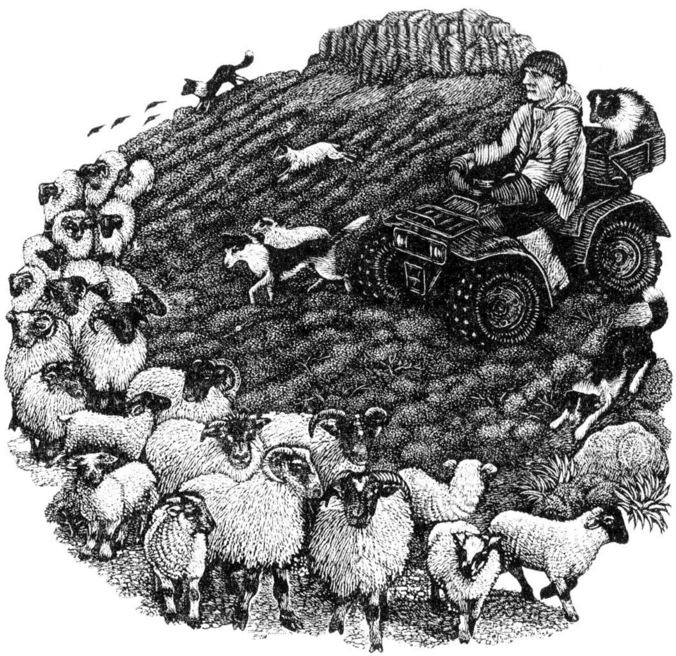

57

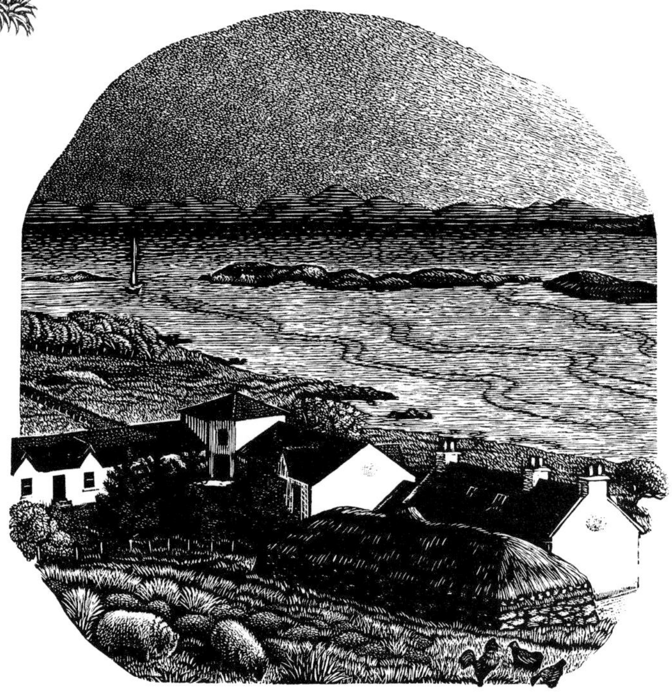

58

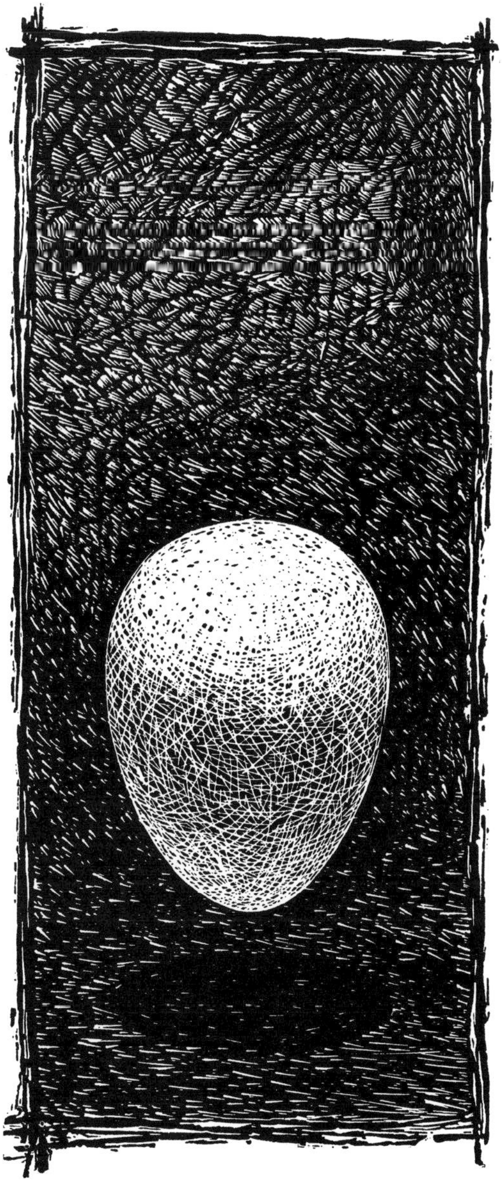

59

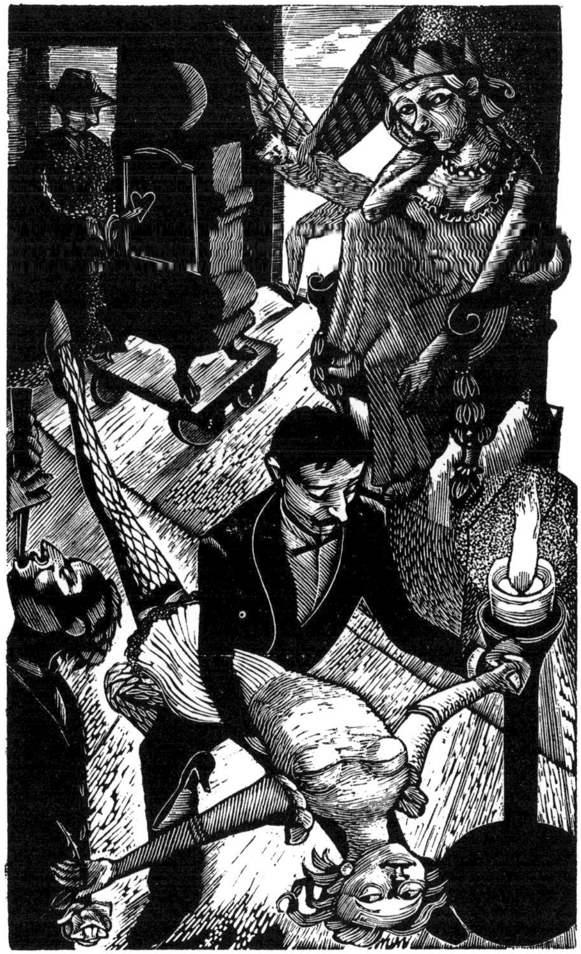

60

from The Society's 2003 Christmas book,
The Most Incredible Thing by Hans Christian Andersen.

61
Miriam Macgregor
*The Rime of the Ancient Mariner**
WOOD ENGRAVING
£70

62
Miriam Macgregor
The Tropic Tree
WOOD ENGRAVING
£65

63 *see page 40*
Hideharu Mishio
Song of the Birds III
MIXED MEDIA
£200

64
M J Mott
Lifeline
WOOD ENGRAVING
£65

65
David Moyer
Landscape with Grub
WOOD ENGRAVING
£90

66
David Moyer
Landscape with Sunflowers
WOOD ENGRAVING
£90

67
Lami Mulvey
Harry
WOOD ENGRAVING
£35

68
Huma Mushtaq
Lamp and Niche
WOOD ENGRAVING
£200

69 *see page 41*
Huma Mushtaq
Parc Guell – Colour
WOOD ENGRAVING
£60

70 *see page 41*
Earl R Nitschke
Three 'Lightning Stones' from Lake Michigan
WOOD ENGRAVING
£45

71
Monika Nykowska
Boat Race II
WOOD CUT
£100

72 *see page 23*
Hilary Paynter
Skern
WOOD ENGRAVING
£60

73
Hilary Paynter
Tree with a Long Memory
WOOD ENGRAVING
£75

74
Hilary Paynter
Carn Brae
PLASTICARD ENGRAVING
£120

75
Pam Pebworth
Kennet & Avon Canal, Bath
WOOD ENGRAVING
£80

* from *Samuel Taylor Coleridge* The Folio Society 2003

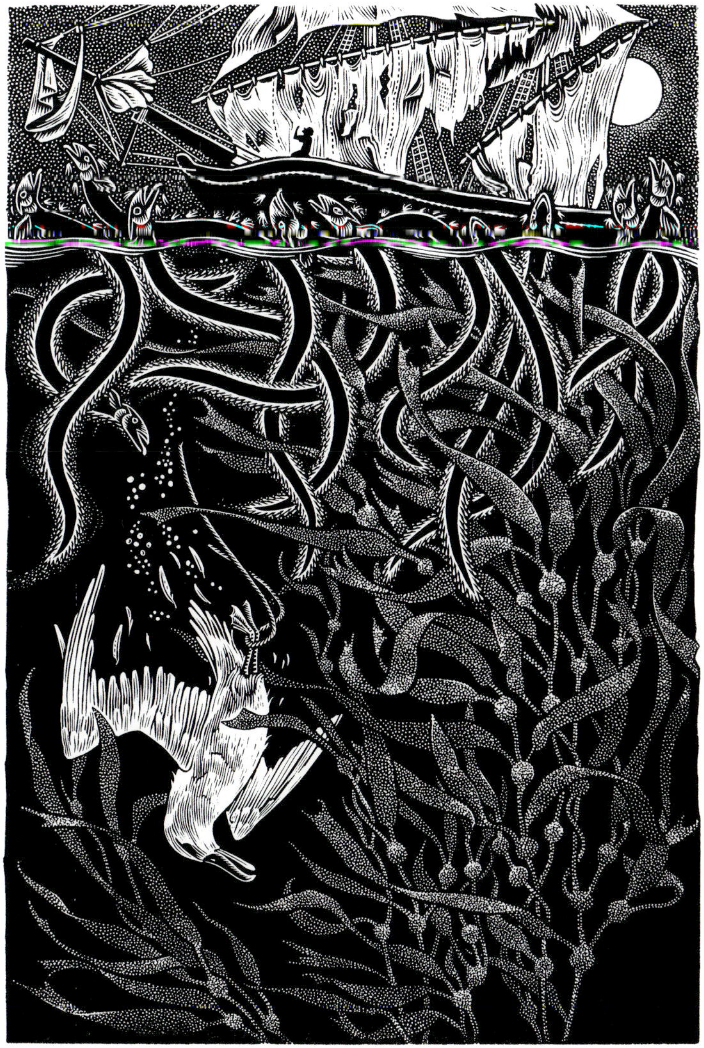

61

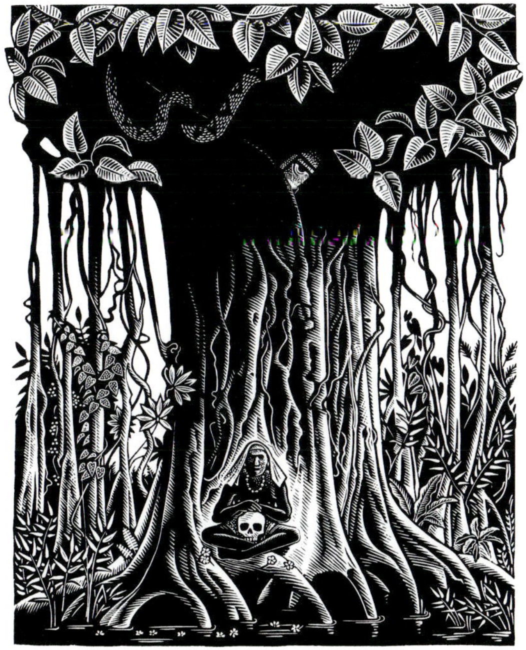

62

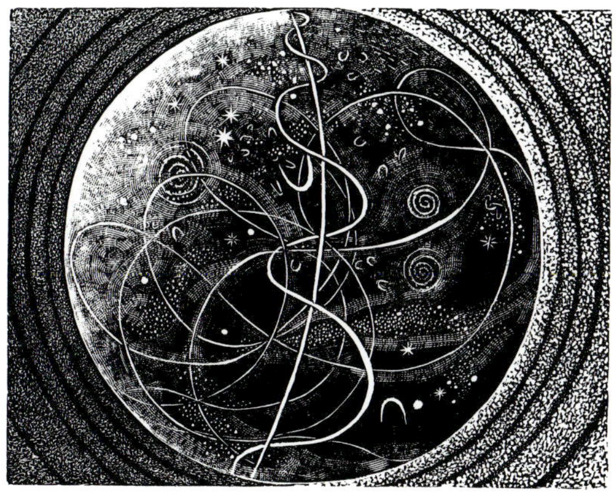

64

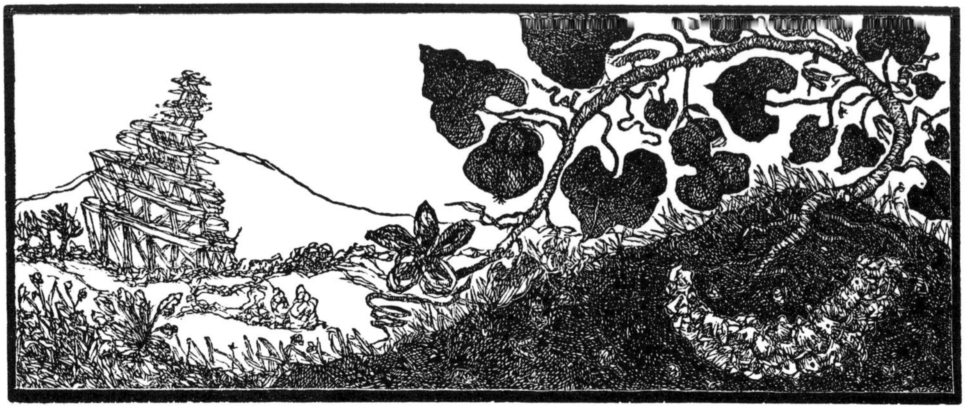

65

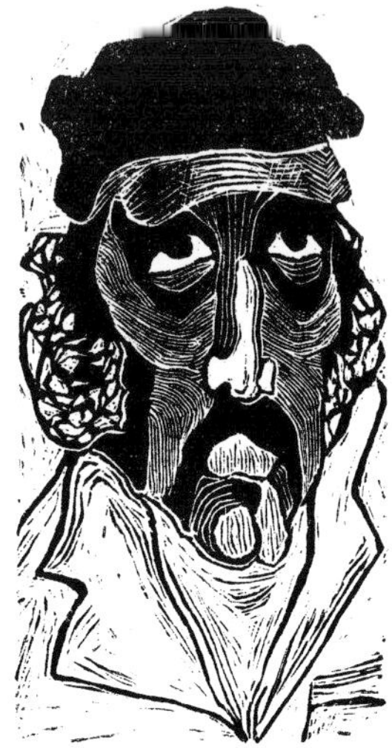

67

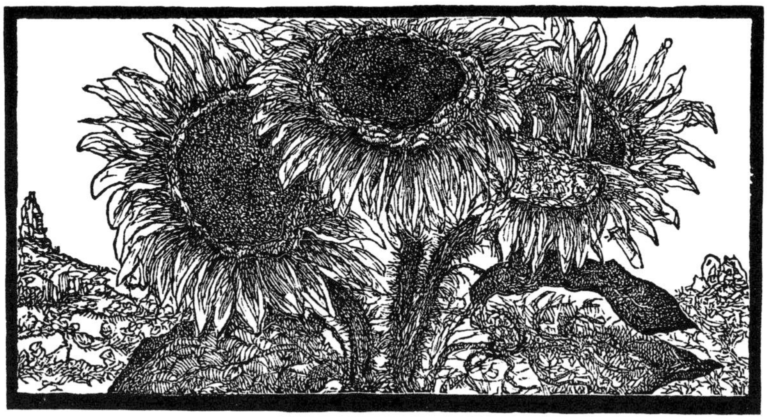

66

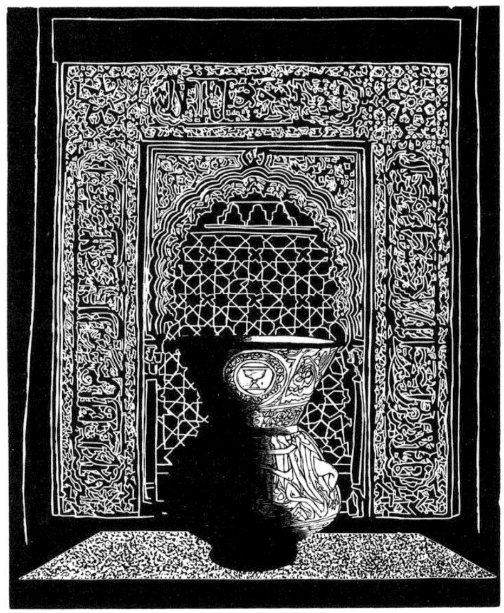

68

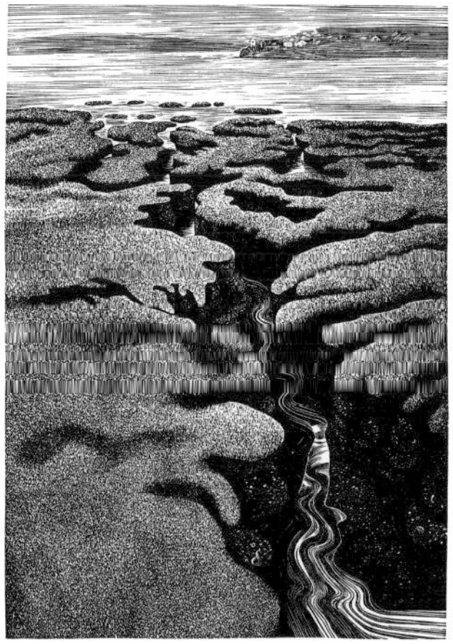

72

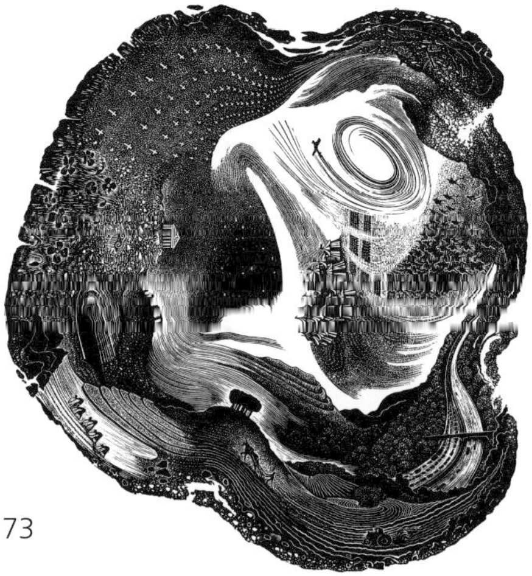

73

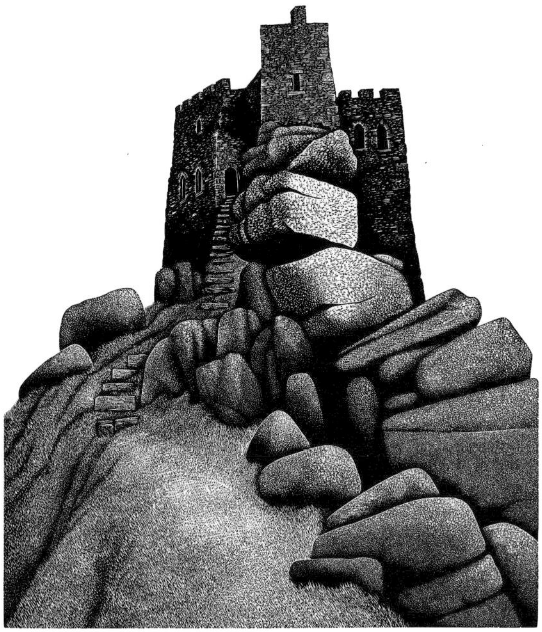

74

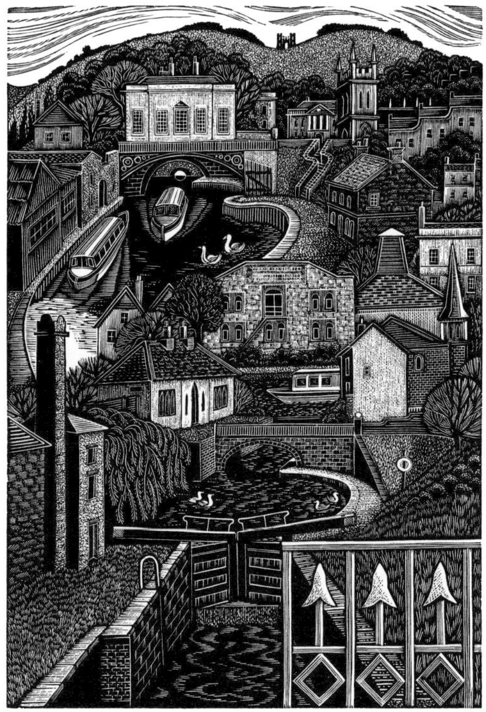

75

76
Howard Phipps
Homington Water Meadows
WOOD ENGRAVING
£95

77
Howard Phipps
Aldeburgh Beach
WOOD ENGRAVING
£95

78
Julian Poole
Chouette
WOOD ENGRAVING
£45

79
Monica Poole
Chalk Rocks
WOOD ENGRAVING
£350

80
Monica Poole
Root
WOOD ENGRAVING
£350

81
Monica Poole
Ripening Corn
WOOD ENGRAVING
£260

82 *see page 41*
Arkady Pugachevsky
Flute
COLOUR ENGRAVING
£150

83
Peter Reddick
Welsh Farm
WOOD ENGRAVING
£60

84
Peter Reddick
Buttermere Revisited
WOOD ENGRAVING
£70

85
Abigail Rorer
Say Cheese
WOOD ENGRAVING
£75

86
Abigail Rorer
Waiting for the Sheep Show
WOOD ENGRAVING
£95

87
Abigail Rorer
Baobabs
WOOD ENGRAVING
£75

88
Mary Rossetti Rutterford
Sherborne Castle & Abbey
WOOD ENGRAVING
£45

89 *see Title page*
Mary Rossetti Rutterford
And You Are?
WOOD ENGRAVING
£40

90
Ronald Salmond
River Windrush at Widford
WOOD ENGRAVING
£60

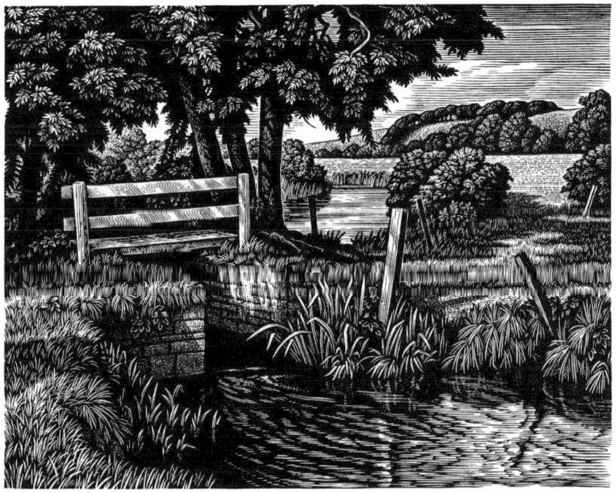

76

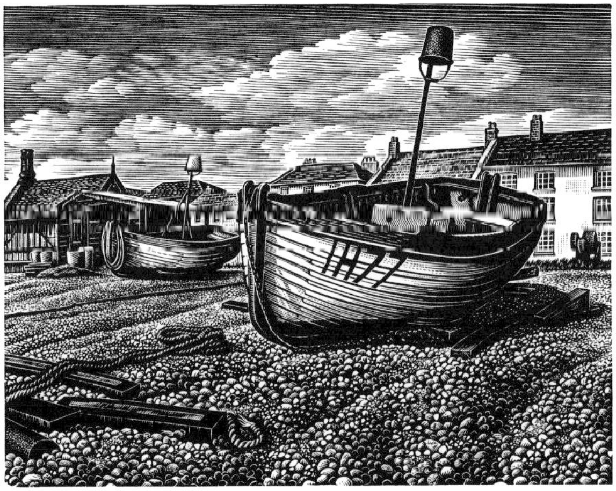

77

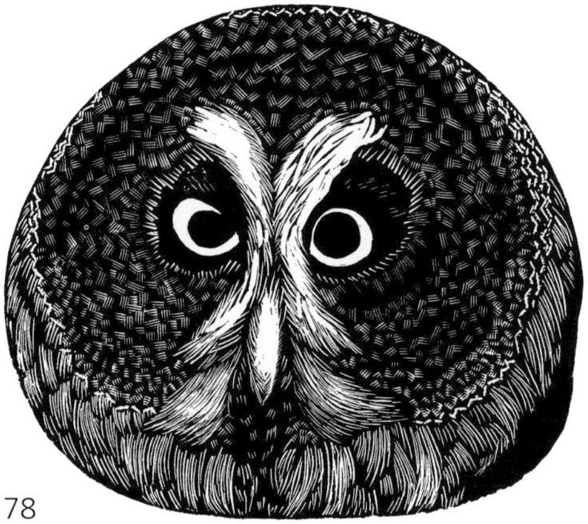

78

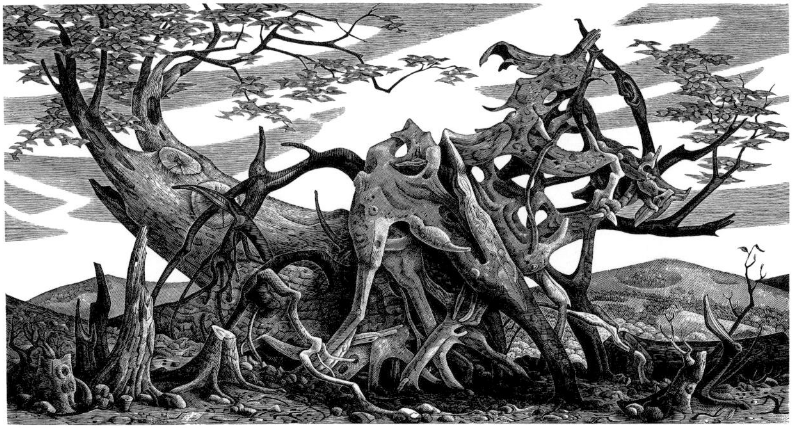

80

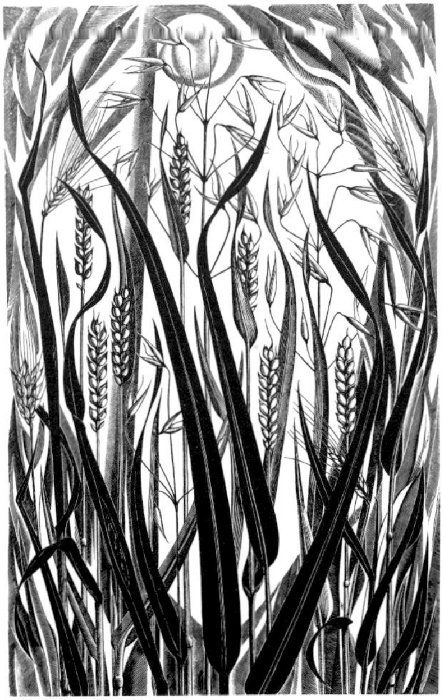

81

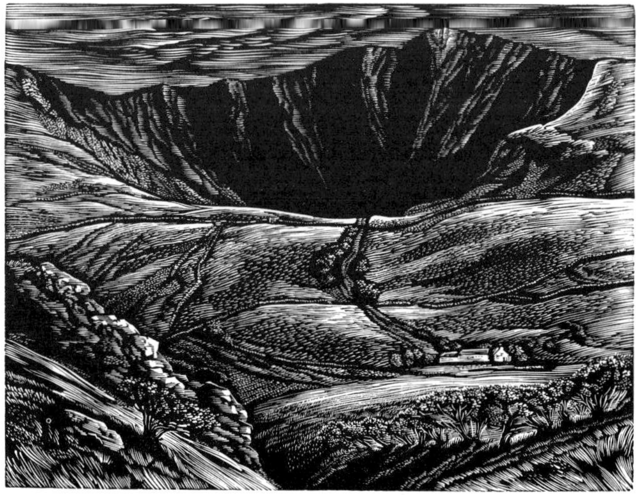

83

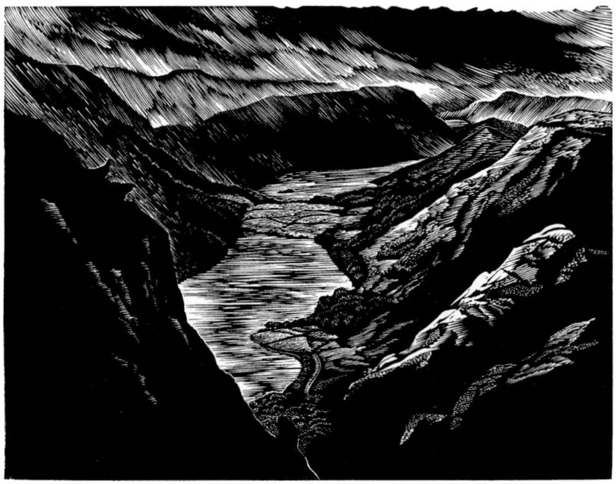

84

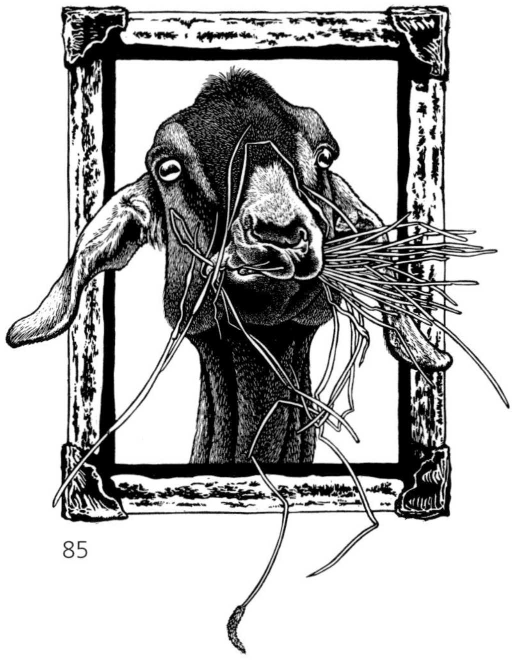

85

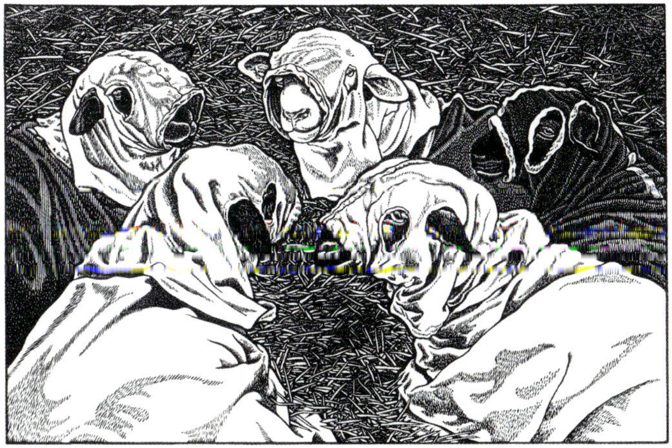

86

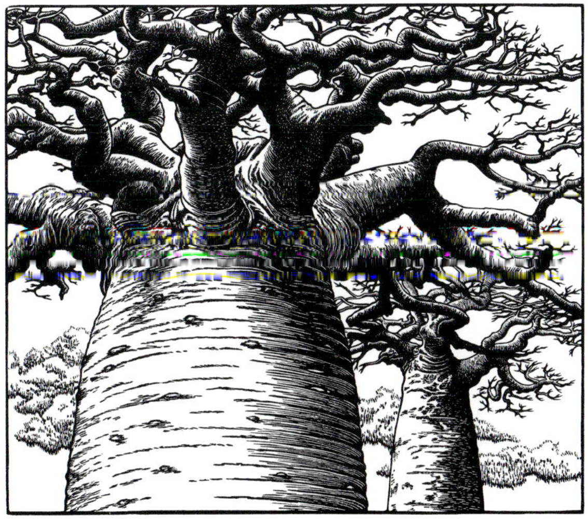

87

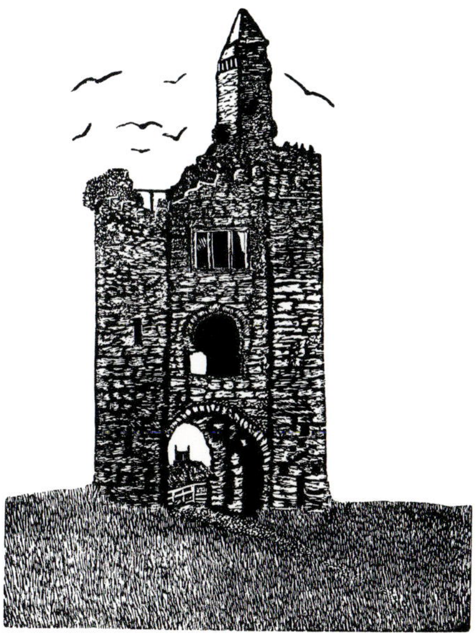

88

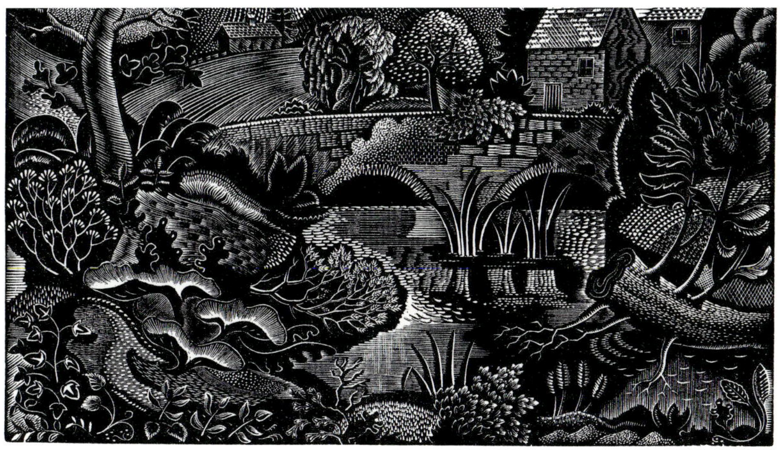

90

91
Ben Sands
Regimental Wet Canteen 1946
LINOCUT
£80

92
Sue Scullard
The Swan, Lavenham
WOOD ENGRAVING
£30

93
Derek Setford
A Brief Encounter
WOOD ENGRAVING
£65

94
Alex Smart
The Cottage – Charlton
WOOD ENGRAVING
Not for Sale

95
Shirley Smith
Alan II France
WOOD ENGRAVING
£45

96
Shirley Smith
St. Joseph's Chapel – Haute Garonne
WOOD ENGRAVING
£50

97 *see page 41*
Thelma K Sykes
InBeTween-Agers
MIXED MEDIA
£210

98
Mary Symons
Fitting Out
WOOD ENGRAVING
£50

99
Margaret Till
The Chiropodist
VINYL ENGRAVING
£20

100
James Todd
Mayakovsky & Lissitsky
WOODCUT
£150

101
Ann Tout
Lemon
WOOD ENGRAVING
£75

102
Ann Tout
The Vicarage
WOOD ENGRAVING
£25

103
Delitza Georgieva Tzoneva
Goat Track
WOOD ENGRAVING
£100

104
Andrei Ushin
First Snow
LINOCUT
£60

105
Nikki Vahle
Picnicing Ants
WOOD ENGRAVING
£70

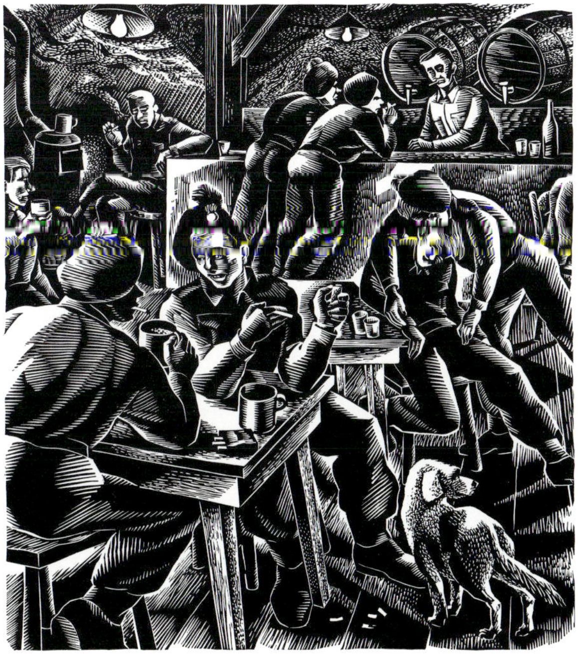

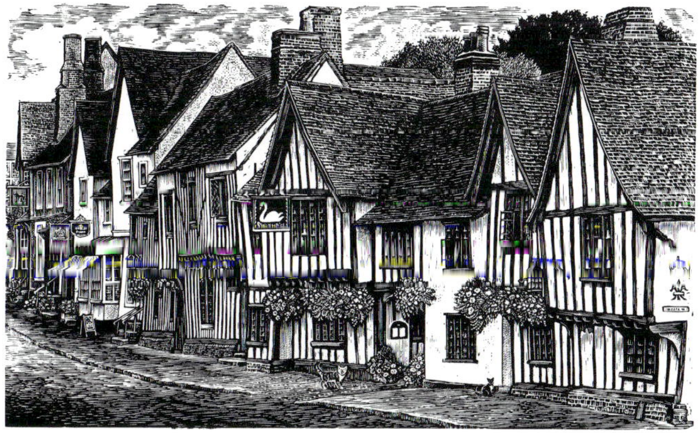

92

91

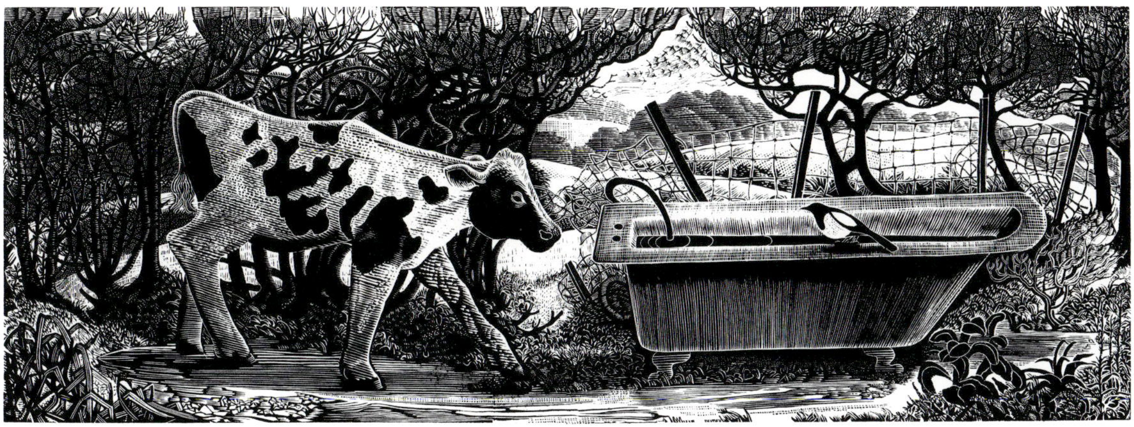

93

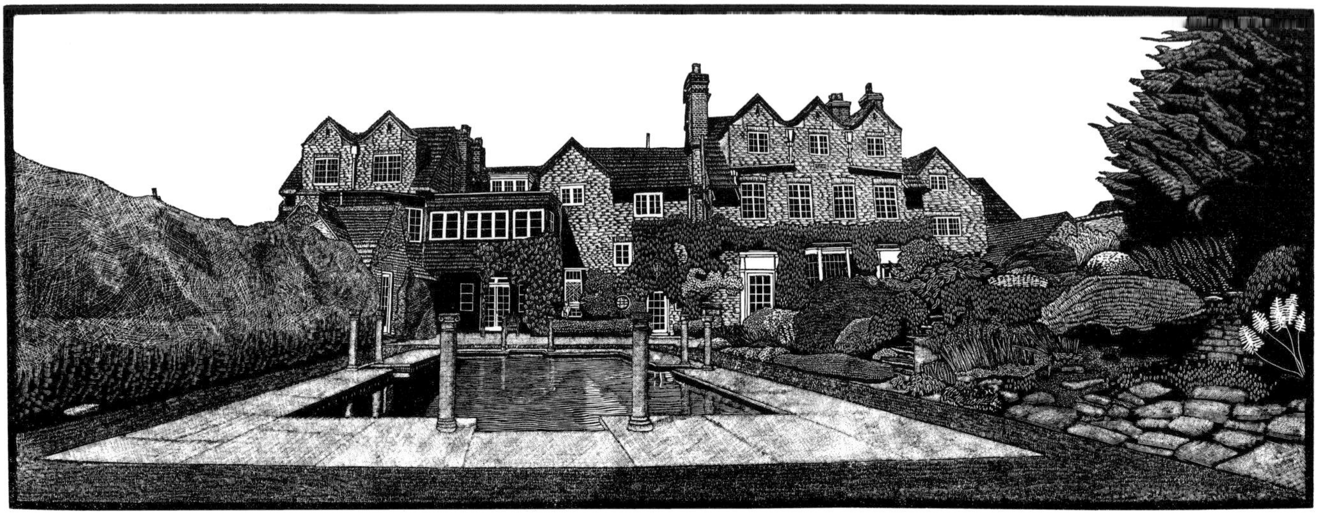

94

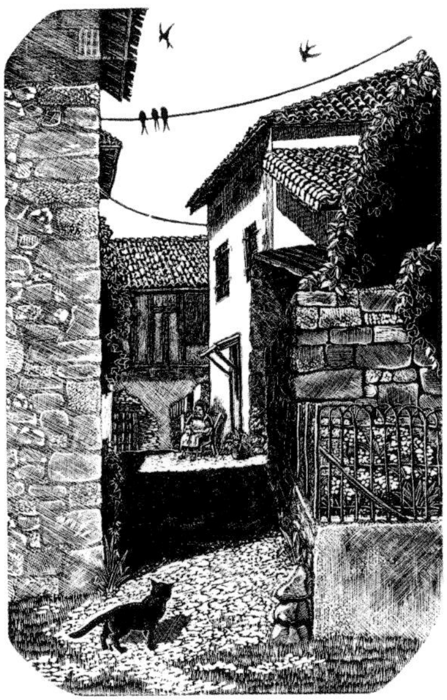

95

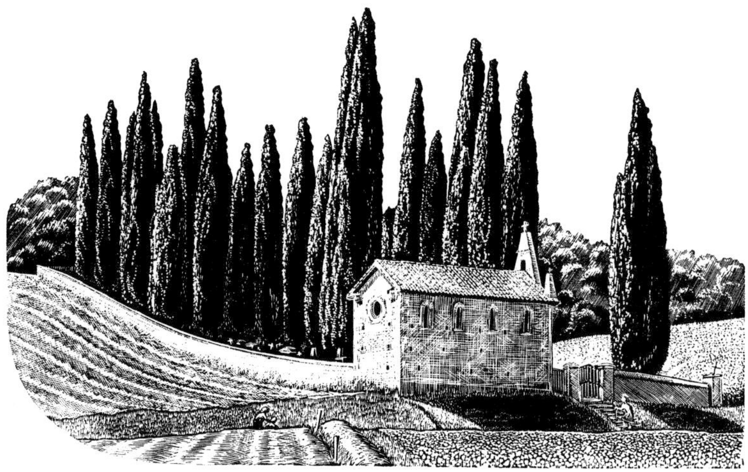

96

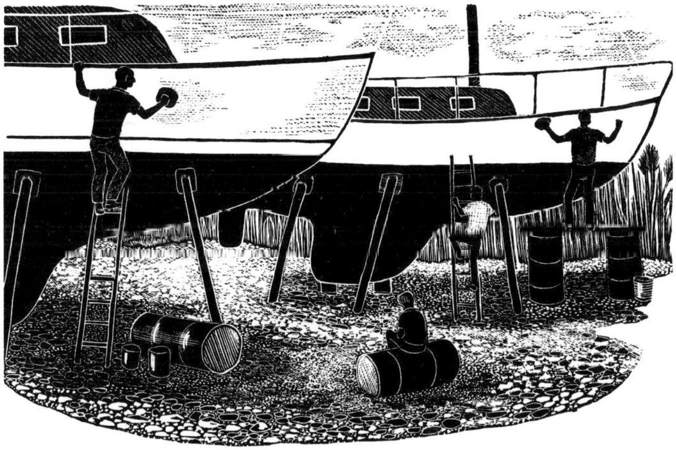

98

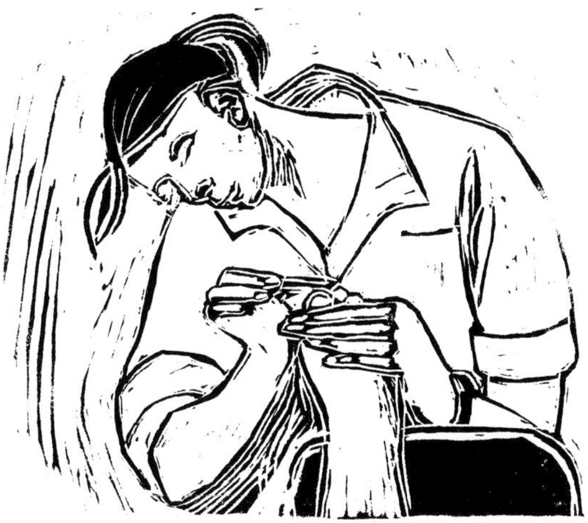

99

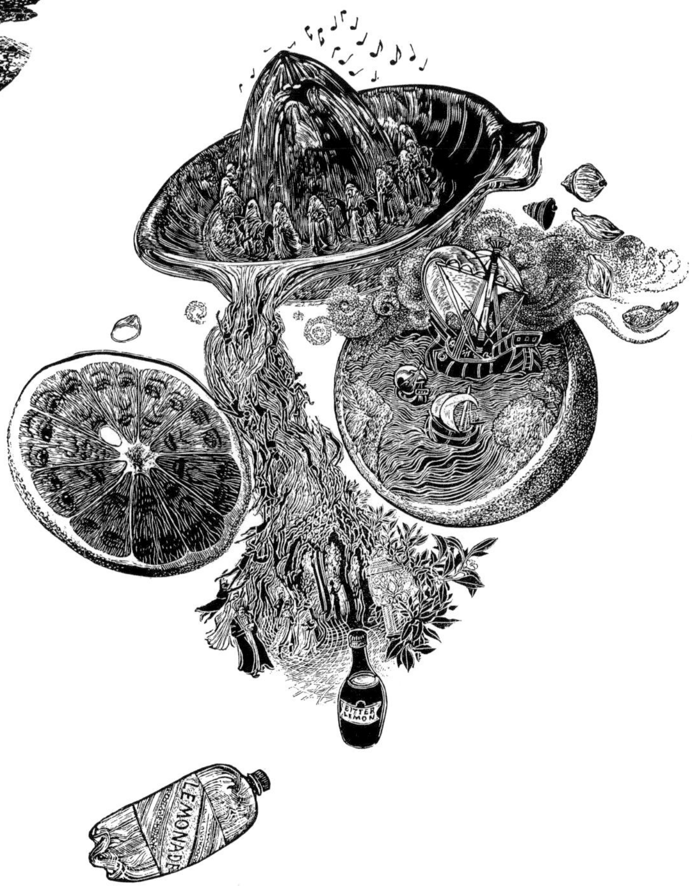

101

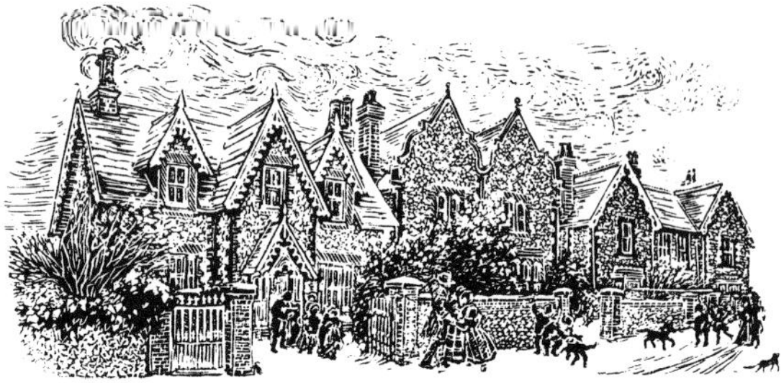

102

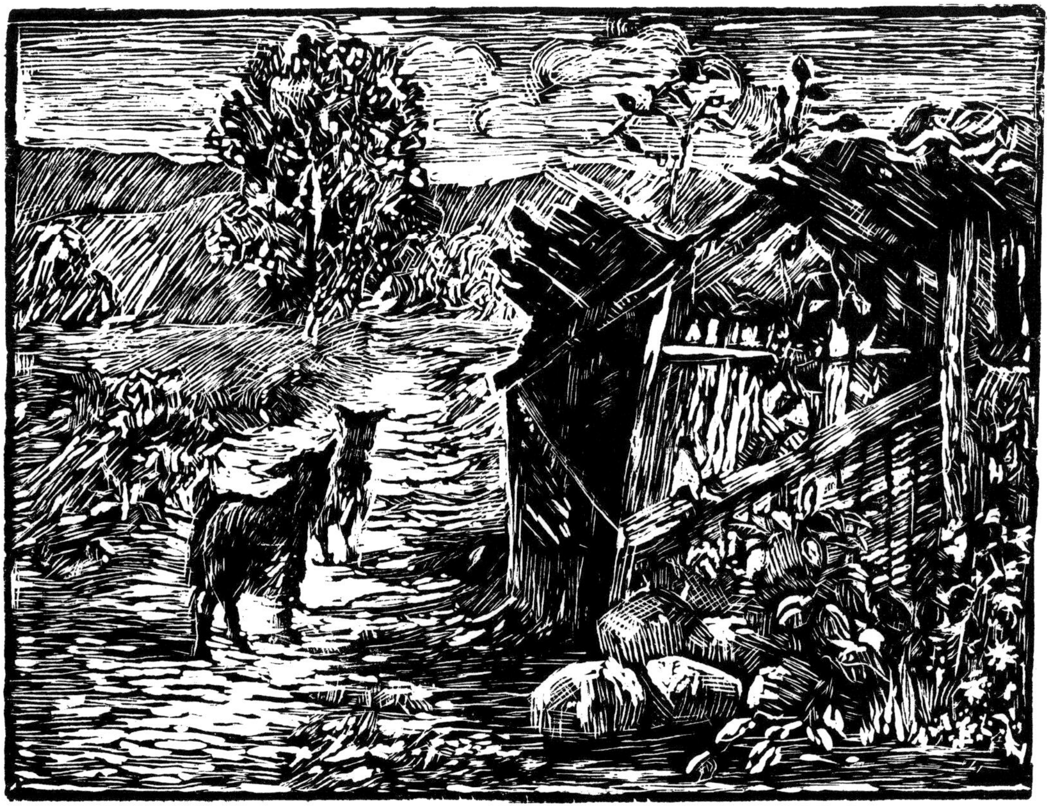

103

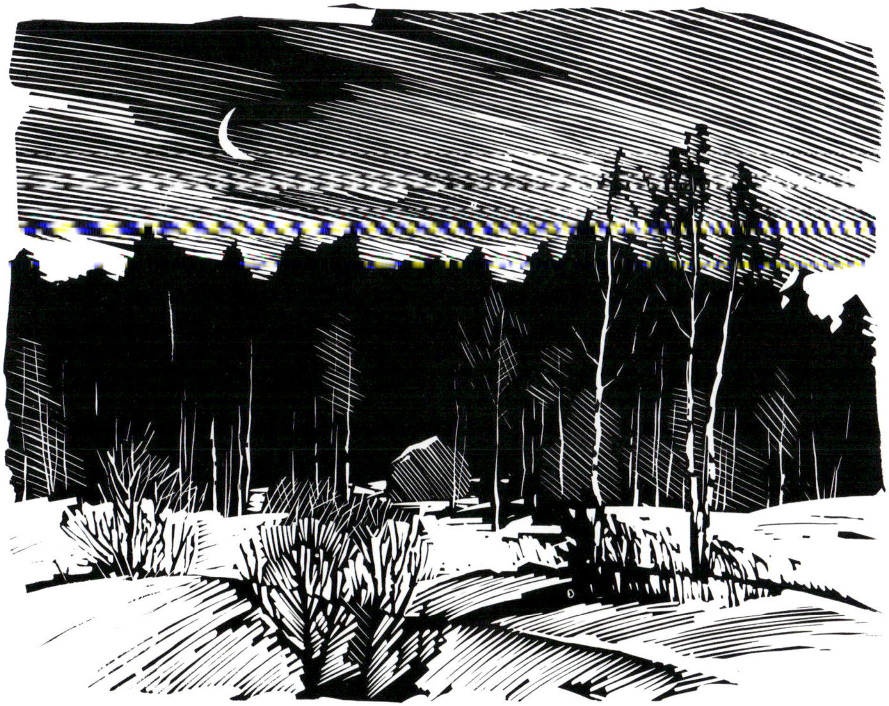

104

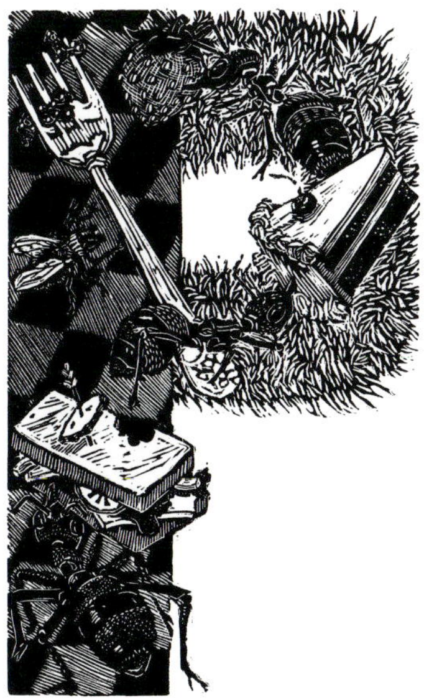

105

106 *see page 13*
Jeroen Van Duyn
Chestnut Tree at Night
WOOD ENGRAVING
£82

107
Sarah Van Niekerk
Conversation in Alan
WOOD ENGRAVING
£100

108
Sarah Van Niekerk
A Day in June
WOOD ENGRAVING
£55

109
Geri Waddington
West Street, Oundle
WOOD ENGRAVING
£80

110
Richard Wagener
Tundra
WOOD ENGRAVING
£180

111
Richard Wagener
Euphorbia Halipedicola
WOOD ENGRAVING
$100

112
Richard Wagener
Manor Porch
WOOD ENGRAVING
$100

113
Sheila Watkins
Fish Leap
WOOD ENGRAVING
£35

114 *see page 42*
John Watson
Rebecca
LINOCUT
£55

115
Jim Westergard
The Artist as Captain Canuck
WOOD ENGRAVING
£90

116
Jim Westergard
The Artist as a Beefeater
WOOD ENGRAVING
£90

117
Jim Westergard
The Artist as a Viking
WOOD ENGRAVING
£90

118
Hilary Wilson
Welsh Terrier Class
WOOD ENGRAVING
£40

119
Barry Woodcock
Mixed Grills
WOOD ENGRAVING
£130

120
Barry Woodcock
Bugs, Gourds and Garlic
WOOD ENGRAVING
£130

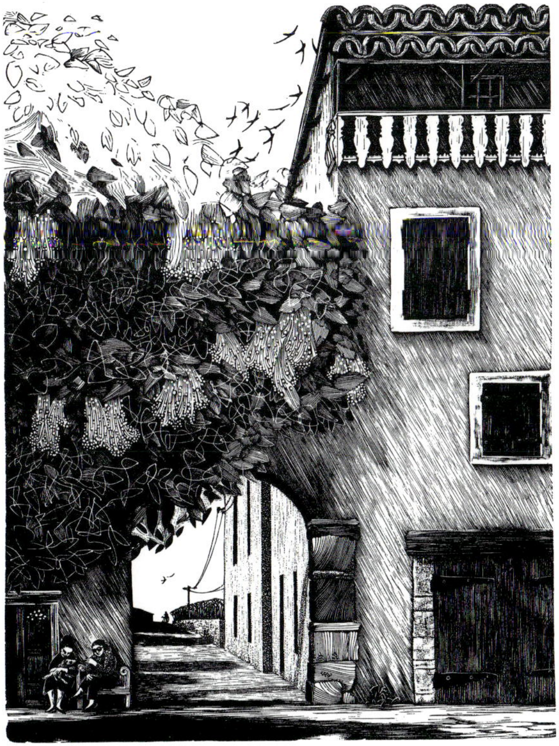

107

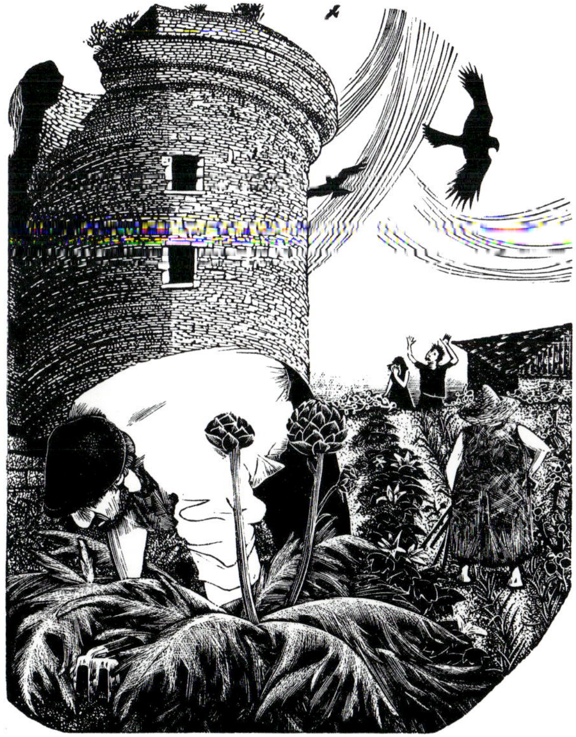

108

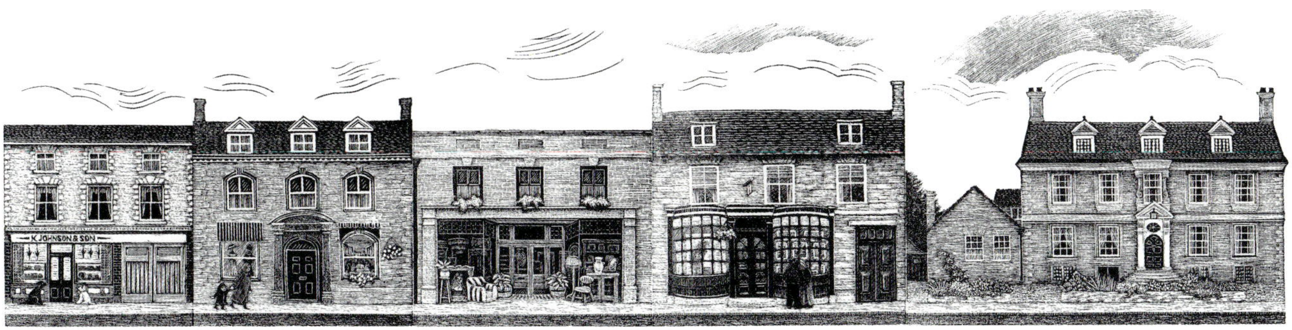

109

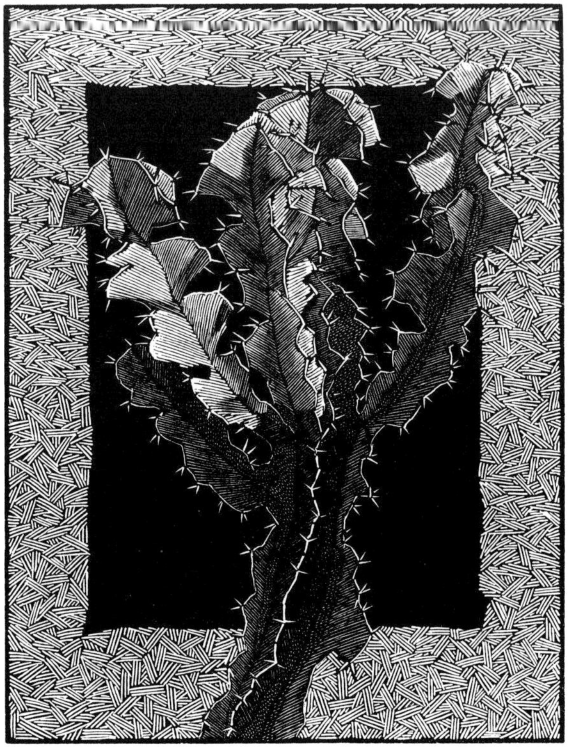

111

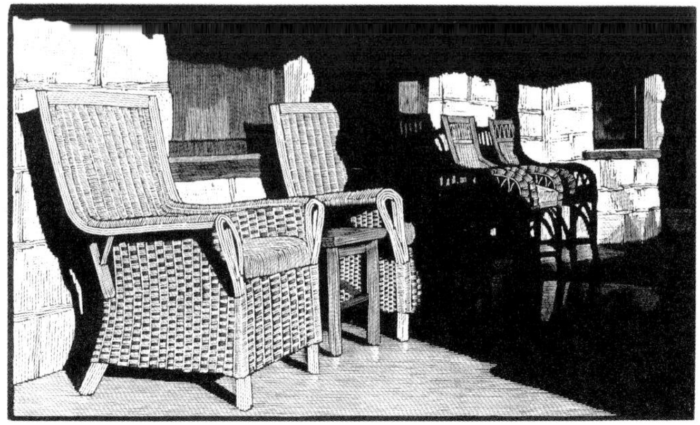

112

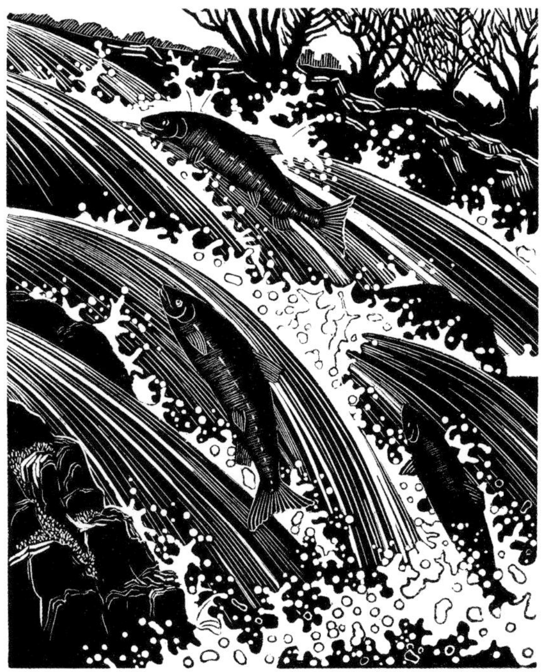

113

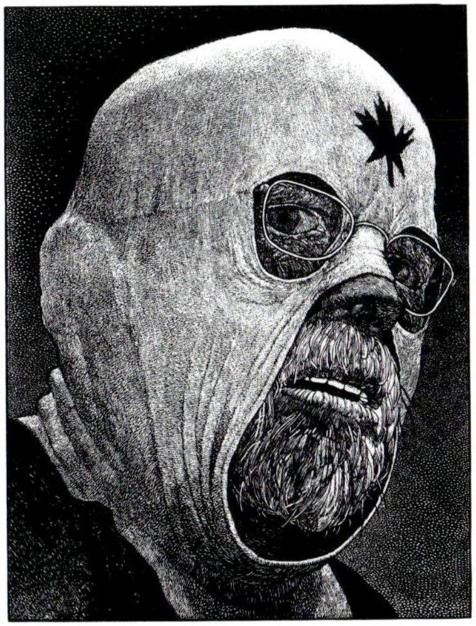

115

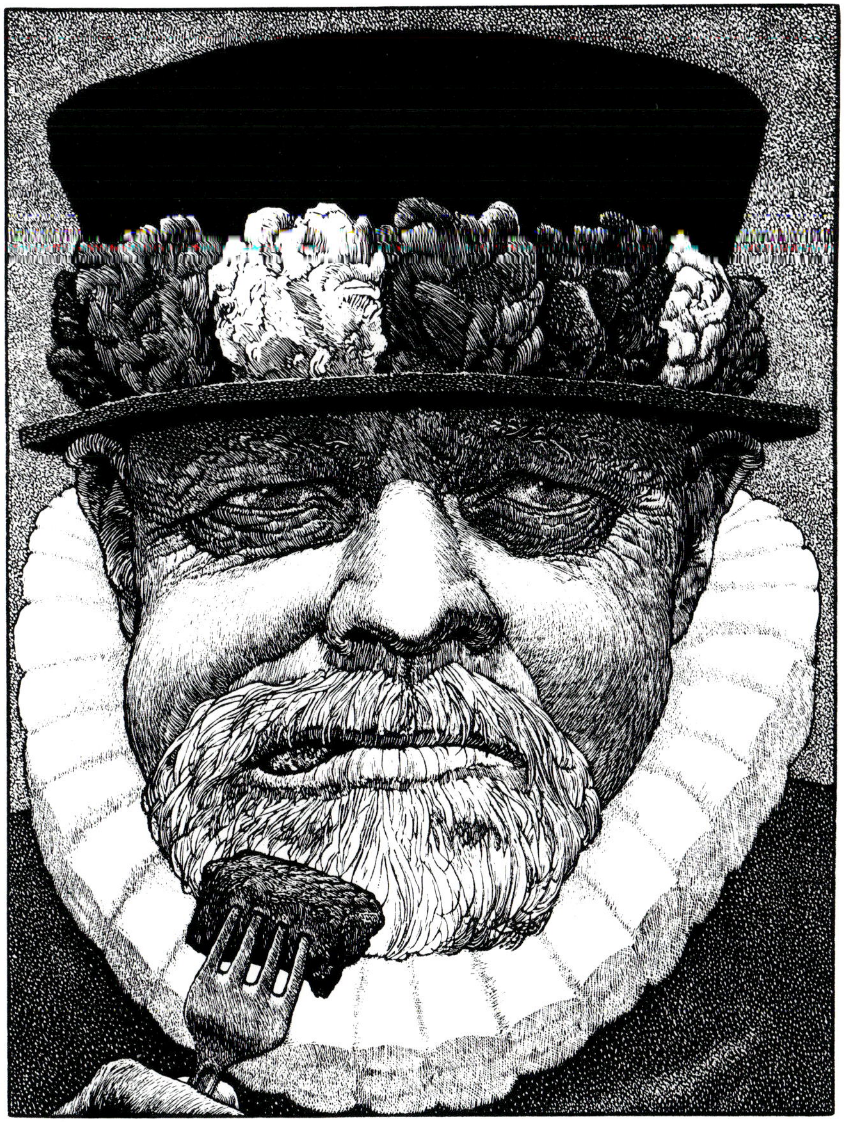

116

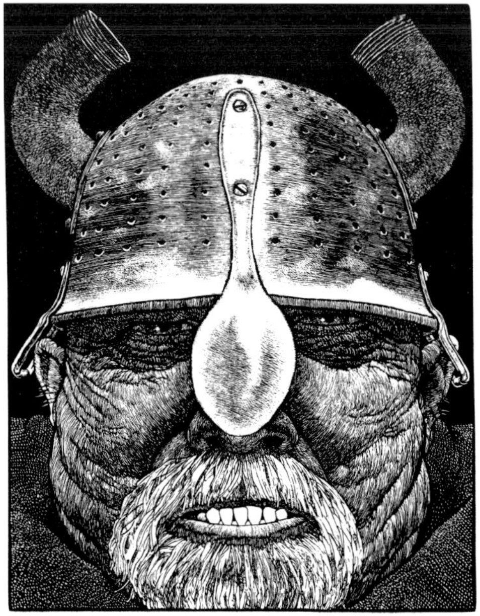

117

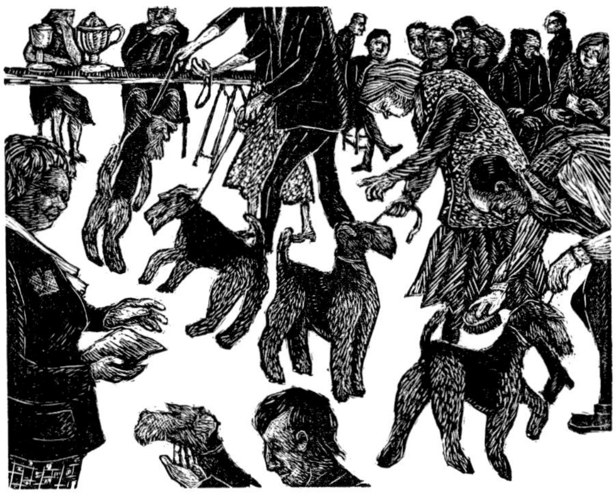

118

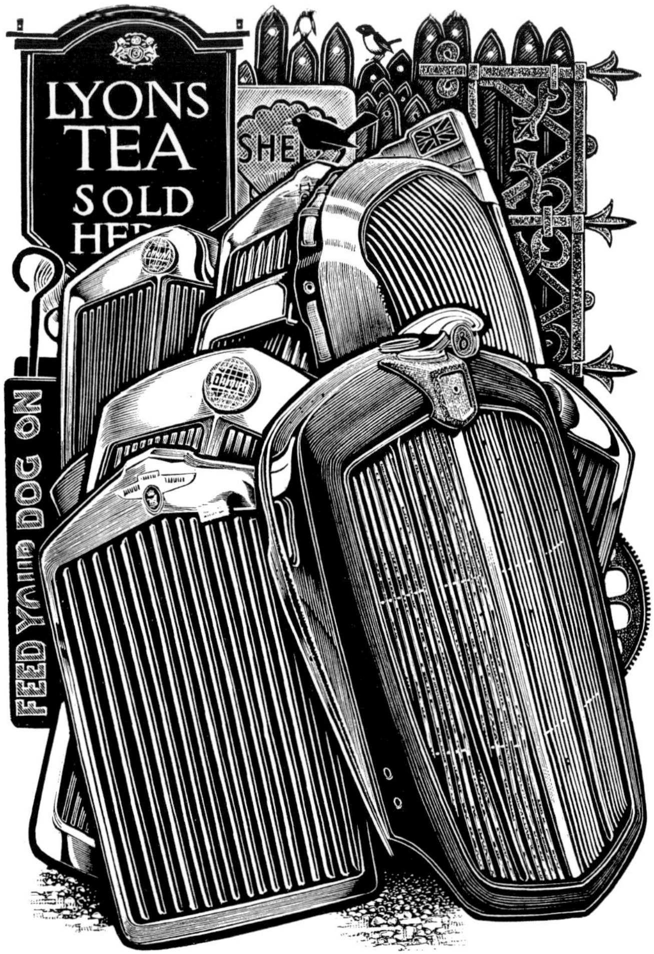

119

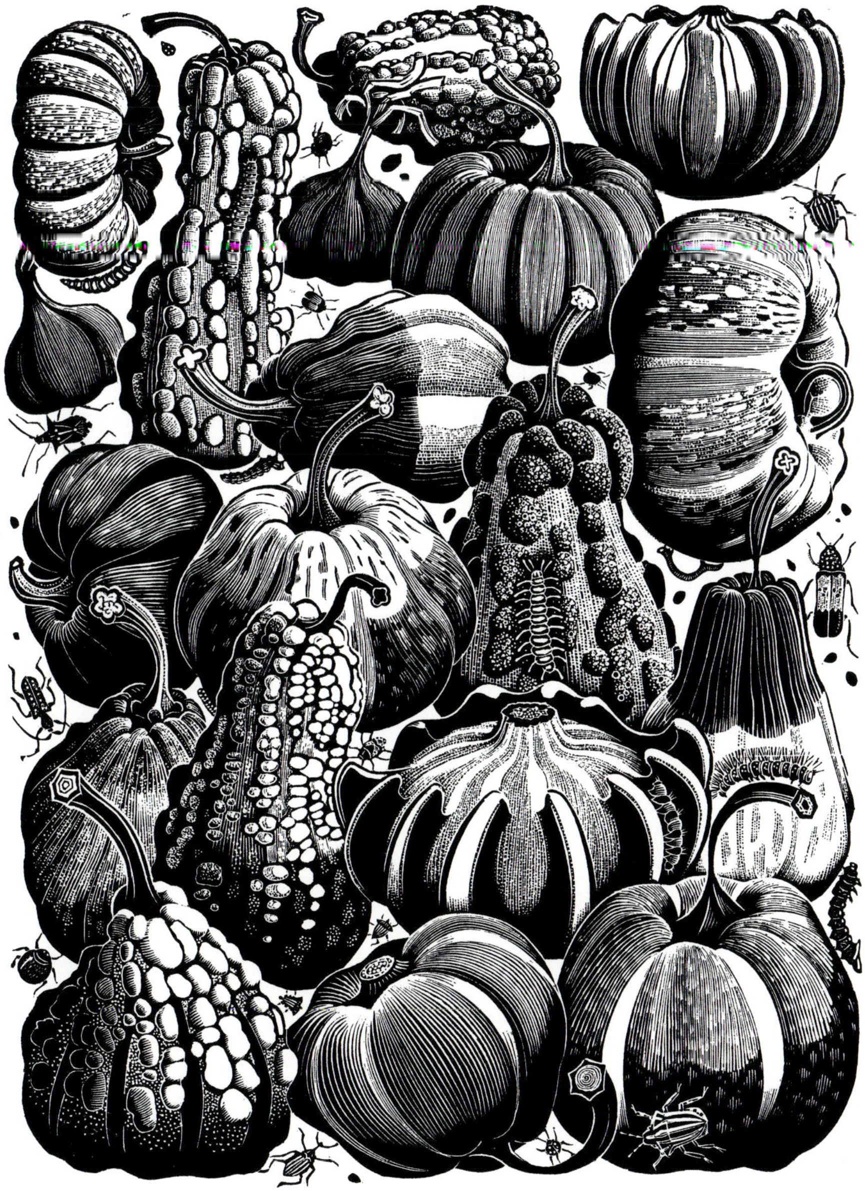

120

PAULA ALLERTON
27 Tudor Road
Hampton
Middlesex TW12 2NG
email: p.allerton@btopenworld.com

MARCUS BEAVEN
1 Moonshine Cottages
The Rocks
Ashwicke
Chippenham
Wilts SN14 8AW
Tel: 01225 859540

RACHEL BECKETT
14 Ardenham Street
Aylesbury
Bucks HP19 8AH
Tel: 01296 427019
email:
rachel@clanbeckett.freeserve.co.uk

MARINA BINDELLA
Via Fonteiana 106
00152 Roma
Italy
Tel: 0039 06 58340774

HUBERT BORYS
Polinezyiska Str. 1/85
02777 Warsaw
Poland
Tel: 00 48 22 644 07 86

SIMON BRETT
12 Blowhorn Street
Marlborough
Wilts SN8 1BT
Tel: 01672 512905

HARRY BROCKWAY
59 Manor House Road
Glastonbury
Somerset BA6 9DF
Tel: 01458 831504

JOHN BRYCE
37 Copse Avenue
Weybourne
Farnham
Surrey GU9 9EA
Tel: 01252 328394

ANNE CATHCART
Fairland
Selmeston
Polegate
East Sussex BN26 6TY
Tel: 01323 811311

SALLY COLE
18 Borlase Close
Helston
Cornwall TR13 8SA
Tel: 01326 562872

A J CUNDALL
Holly Cottage
8 Oxen Road
Crewkerne
Somerset TA18 7HN
Tel: 01460 73168

CLAIRE DALBY
2 West Park
Stanley
Perthshire PH1 4QH
Tel: 01738 827222

CHRIS DAUNT
1 Monkridge Gardens
Dunston
Gateshead NE11 9XE
Tel: 0191 4208975
email: chris_daunt@blueyonder.co.uk

DANIEL DENNISON
8 Millpond Avenue
Hayle
Cornwall SY23 1PU
email: ddd9@aber.ac.uk

ANNE DESMET
22 Queen Anne Road
Hackney
London E9 7AH
Tel: 020 8533 0235

KATE DICKER
6 Rosewarne Court
Hyde Street
Winchester
Hants SO23 7HL
Tel: 01962 869617
email: Kd@zappypod.fsnet.uk

ANTHONY DUNIGAN
26 Whiting Road
Oulton
Lowestoft
Suffolk NR32 3QA
Tel: 01502 501434

ANDY ENGLISH

92 Cannon Street
Little Downham
Ely
Cambridgeshire CB6 2SS
Tel: 01353 699657
email: a.english@virgin.net

RICHARD M FRANKLIN

Rütimeyerstrasse 33
CH-4054 Basel
Switzerland
Tel: 00 4161 271 4648
email: Richard.Franklin@unibas.ch

RAYMOND GLOECKLER

305 Riverview Court
Portage
Wisconsin 53901
USA
Tel: 00 608 745 4989

DAVID HACKMAN

18 Eve Road
Isleworth
Middlesex TW7 7HS

TREVOR HADDRELL

Woodwell Cottage
White Hart Steps
Clifton Wood
Bristol BS8 4TQ
Tel: 0117 929 8363

ANNE HAYWARD

Yew Tree Cottage
Outlands Lane
Curdridge
Hants SO30 2HD
Tel: 01489 781618

H J JACKSON

12 Whitehall Road
Norwich NR2 3EW
Tel: 01603 611848

PAULINE JACOBSEN

Thornhill
Cults
Aberdeen AB15 9QJ
Tel: 01224 867238

JUDY JAIDINGER

6110 N. Newburg Ave.
Chicago IL 60631
USA
Tel: 00 1 773 774 7689
email: jaidinger@worldnet.att.net

RIE KAWAUCHI

4-2-17 Akazutsumi
Setagaya-Ku,
Tokyo 156-0044
Japan
Fax: 00 81 3 3324 8233

GILLIAN KENNY

Pear House
Stone Hill
Sellindge
Ashford
Kent TN25 6EW
Tel: 01303 812147

PAUL L KERSHAW

Altvaid
Harlosh
Dunvegan
Isle of Skye IV55 8ZF
Tel: 01470 521288
email: plk@plkershaw.co.uk

ROSEMARY KILBOURN

18620 Centreville Creek Road
R.R.1. Caledon East
Ontario L0N 1E0
Canada

CELINA KIRCHNER

Ul.Szeroka 23/1A
40231 Katowice
Poland

JOHN LAWRENCE

6 Worts Causeway
Cambridge CB1 8RL
Tel: 01223 247449

PETER LAWRENCE

48 Lonsdale Road
Oxford OX2 7EP
Tel: (H)01865 559193
(W)01865 512331
email: pete@odi-design.co.uk

PETER LAZAROV

Zilverlaan 127
9743RG Groningen
Holland
email: peterr@lazarov.nl

KATHLEEN LINDSLEY

10 Lower Milovaig
Glendale
Dunvegan
Isle of Skye IV55 8WR
Tel: 01470 511367
email: raven@kathleenlindsley.co.uk

SUSAN LOWDERMILK

812 W 22nd Avenue
Eugene
Oregon 97405
USA

Tel: 00 1 541-242 6968
Fax: 00 1 541-463 4185
email: lowdermilks@lanecc.edu

JANE LYDBURY

101 Humber Road
London SE3 7LW

MIRIAM MACGREGOR

30 Whittington Village
Cheltenham
Gloucestershire GL54 4HD

Tel: 01242 820892

HIDEHARU MISHIO

11-21-304 Ogino
Yokosuka-shi
Kanagawa 240 0102
Japan

Tel: 00 81 44 468 56 6110

M J MOTT

Windrush
Great Waldingfield
Sudbury
Suffolk CO10 0RZ

Tel: 01787 210419
Fax: 01787 210808
email: mj_mott@compuserve.com

DAVID MOYER

205 S Market Street
Muncy
PA 17556
USA

email: redhowler@alltel.net

LAMI MULVEY

33 Regent Place
Edinburgh EH7 5BG

Tel: 0131 661 7750
email: mulvey@ednet.co.uk

HUMA MUSHTAQ

18 Healey Avenue
High Wycombe
Bucks HP13 7JP
email: huma01uk@yahoo.co.uk

EARL R NITSCHKE

1324 East Bennett Street
Mount Pleasant
Michigan
MI 48858
USA

Tel: 00 1 989 773 9030

MONIKA NYKOWSKA

UL. W. Gombrowieza 11/16
Czestochowa 42-200

Tel: 00 48 34 3622570

HILARY PAYNTER

Torridge House
Torridge Hill
Bideford
Devon EX39 2AZ

Tel/fax: 01237 479679
email: hilary@paynter.co.uk

PAM PEBWORTH

Dovetail
Lower Town
Samford Peverell
Tiverton
Devon EX16 7EG

Tel: 01884 820505

HOWARD PHIPPS

Hilfield
Homington Road
Coombe Bissett
Salisbury
Wilts SP5 4ND

Tel: 01722 718294

JULIAN POOLE

Longchalks
The Chalks
Chew Magna
Bristol BS40 8SN

email: jandapoole@waitrose.com

MONICA POOLE

c/o Hilary Paynter
Torridge House
Torridge Hill
Bideford
Devon EX39 2AZ

Tel/fax: 01237 479679
email: hilary@paynter.co.uk

ARKADY PUGACHEVSKY

Entusiastov Str 33-102
02147 Kiev
Ukraine

Tel: 00 380 44 555 4459
email: dmdc@i.com.ua

PETER REDDICK

18 Hartington Park
Bristol BS6 7ES

Tel: 0117 924 9167
email: reddickpeter@waitrose.com

ABIGAIL RORER

16 Oliver Street
Petesham
Massachusetts 01366
USA

Tel: 00 1 978 724 6672
email: loneoakpr49@earthlink.net

MARY ROSSETTI RUTTERFORD
Red House
Waterloo Lane
Stourton Caundle
Sturminster Newton
Dorset DT10 2JF
Tel: 01963 362534
email: l.rutterford@btopenworld.com

RONALD SALMOND
13 Treve Avenue
Harrow
Middlesex HA1 4AL
Tel: 020 8422 6841

BEN SANDS
97 Island Wall
Whitstable
Kent CT5 1EL
Tel: 01227 261155

SUE SCULLARD
Beech Hill Cottage
Glassenbury Road
Cranbrook
Kent TN17 2QJ
Tel: 01580 714340
email: sue@scullard.fsnet.co.uk

DEREK SETFORD
1 Oakbank Drive
Sharples
Bolton
Lancs BL1 7DG
Tel: 01204 303178

ALEX SMART
Three Acres
Pimlico
Brackley
Northants NN13 5TN
Tel: 01280 850547

SHIRLEY SMITH
Wyncroft
2 Rydon Acres
Stoke Gabriel
Totnes
Devon TQ9 6QJ
Tel: 01803 782739
email:
shirleysmith@sagainternet.co.uk

THELMA K SYKES
Blue Neb Studios
18 Newcroft
Saughall
Chester CH1 6EL
Tel: 01244 880209
email: thelmasykes@tiscali.co.uk

MARY SYMONS
Stella Cottage
1 Camp Hill
Farnham
Surrey GU10 1RJ
Tel: 01252 782208

MARGARET TILL
14 Western Hill
Durham DH1 4RL
Tel: 0191 3847129

JAMES TODD
6917 Siesta Drive
Missoula
Montana 59802
USA

ANN TOUT
7 St Catherine's Way
Fareham
Hants PO16 8RL
Tel: 01329 280688

DELITZA GEORGIEVA TZONEVA
No. 6
16 St Zvezdiza
9103 Varna
Bulgaria
Tel: 00 359 52 725368

ANDREI USHIN
c/o Off Centre Gallery
13 Cotswold Road
Bristol BS3 4NX
Tel: 0117 987 2647
email: offcentre@lineone.net

NIKKI VAHLE
700 E Pinewood Avenue
Seward
NE 68434
USA
email: navahle@uwalumni.com

JEROEN VAN DUYN
Coffray
Flety 58170
France
Tel: 00 33 38 630 8195

SARAH VAN NIEKERK
Priding House
Saul
Gloucestershire GL2 7LG
Tel: 01452 740285

GERI WADDINGTON
3 West Street
Oundle
Northants PE8 4EJ
Tel: 01832 275028
email: g.waddington@dial.pipex.com

RICHARD WAGENER

3675 Longview Valley Road
Sherman Oaks
California 91423
USA

email: mxlydian@mindspring.com

SHEILA WATKINS

Hayescroft
Grants Lane
Wincanton
Somerset BA9 9LY

JOHN WATSON

17 Bonnyrigg Road
Eskbank
Midlothian
Scotland EH22 3HA

JIM WESTERGARD

14 Munro Crescent
Red Deer
Alberta
Canada T4N 0JI

Tel: 00 1 403 343 1772
email: jimwest@telusplanet.net

HILARY WILSON

44A Sauncey Avenue
Harpenden
Herts AL5 4QL

Tel: 01582 712243

BARRY WOODCOCK

19 Bayard Avenue
Brightlingsea
Essex CO7 0NH

Tel: 01206 304756

MONICA POOLE 1921–2003: A TRIBUTE

to accompany the special display of her work at the Bankside Gallery

Monica Poole was born in Kent and lived there all her life. Her education at Thanet and the Central Schools of Art was interrupted by the Second World War and, in the years of her young adulthood and maturity, she lived through the most difficult years for wood engraving, when the subject almost vanished. Others of her generation sought after outlets, in teaching, in other forms of printmaking, in the illustrational and commercial work which are also a vital part of wood engraving. None kept faith with wood engraving as a printmaker's art so single-mindedly or persistently as she. None worked the

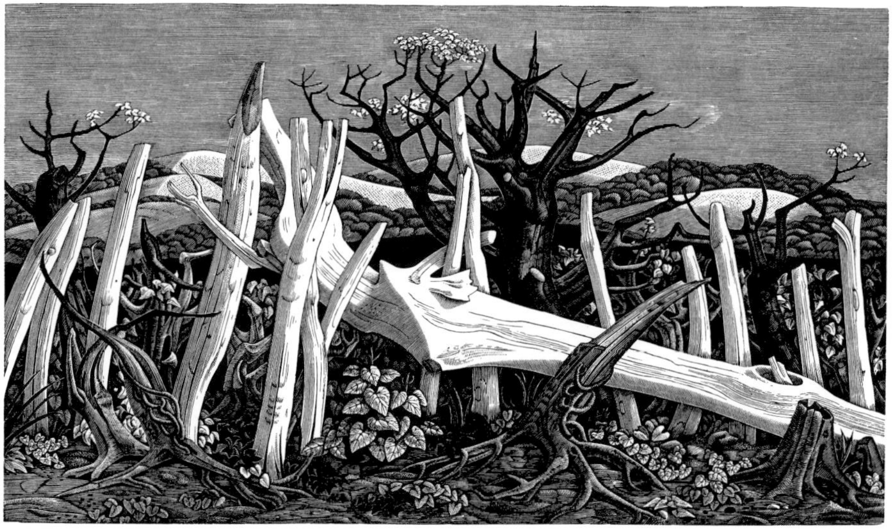

Old Fence

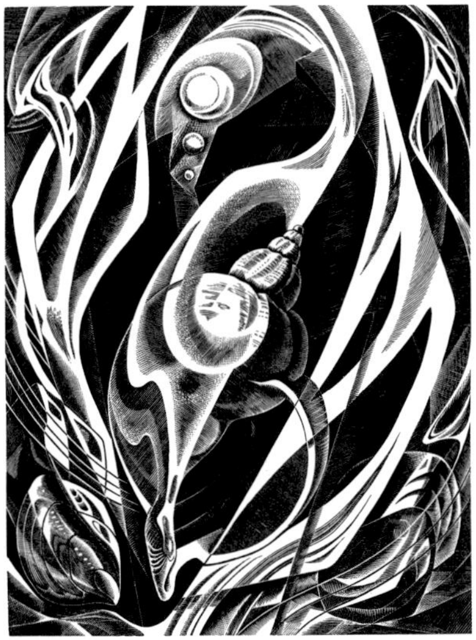

Shell

medium with such refined understanding of its potential. None used it to create so singular and distilled a vision, limiting that potential precisely to what expressed her own temperament. Monica's perception of the chalk downs of her native country, its shores and quarries and plant-life, and the dried husks of nature found there, seemed as natural as breathing to her. It was the material for a visual language of chastening austerity and cool, sub-lunar richness, bordering at times on the surreal.

Monica Poole was elected an associate of the Royal Society of Painter-Etchers and Engravers, as it was then called, in 1967 and a Fellow in 1976; she became a member of the Art Workers Guild in 1970; and joined the Society of Wood Engravers when it re-formed in 1984. She exhibited regularly at the RE and at the Royal Academy over many years. A small series of distinguished solo exhibitions, from the 1980s on, culminated in a major retrospective at the Ashmolean Museum in Oxford in 1993. She died on August 3, 2003, and will be hugely missed.

Simon Brett

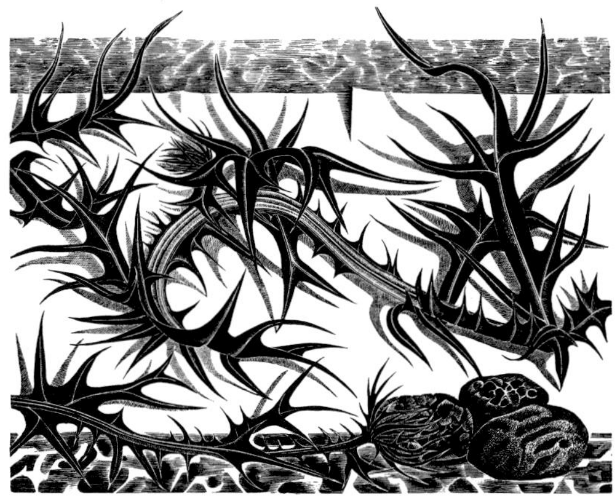

Still Life

ABOUT THE SOCIETY

A historical footnote to the article on p. 12

"Engraving Then and Now ... *was the fiftieth exhibition since [the Society's] original foundation in 1920.*"

The Society was founded by Robert Gibbings, Eric Gill, Gwen Raverat, John Nash and others in Philip Hagreen's studio in 1920. The cultural climate was considerably changed by the 1928 depression and, by 1939, it was not only the advent of war but a sense of having run out of steam that led to the proclamation of the end of an era. Had the sequence of annual shows been uninterrupted, the 50th exhibition would, of course, have been in 1970; but the Second World War broke the pattern, which then lapsed again during the 1960s and '70s, making the 50th exhibition some seventeen years late. *Engraving Then and Now* was held at the old Conduit Street Galleries of the Royal Society of Painter-Printmakers, by then owned by Sotheby's.

The Society's thirty-year, post-war history is less written about but admirable work was produced. To quote an earlier catalogue: 'The 1940s and '50s were hardly a barren period if it saw the later works of [Gertrude] Hermes and [Blair] Hughes-Stanton, the work of George Mackley, the late Sussex landscapes of Clifford Webb, all the major prints of John Farleigh, a good three-quarters of Agnes Miller Parker's engraving, all of Claire Leighton's American work, Monica Poole, Frank Martin and the first engravings of George Tute.' Joan Hassall and Reynolds Stone should also be mentioned. It would be fair to say, though, that much of this work was in the emotional mode of earlier decades rather than having found a voice proper to wood engraving yet speaking to current feeling, as is the case today, especially when the subject is viewed internationally.

ABOUT THE SOCIETY

The Society of Wood Engravers today

BECOME A SUBSCRIBER

Anyone may subscribe to the Society, which is much more than just being on a mailing list: it is in a real sense to be a supporter and friend. Subscribers receive the Society's newsletter *Multiples*, currently issued every other month, and a warm welcome to private views and other events such as the annual picnic. Subscriptions: £25 p.a. in the UK and Europe; £35 overseas.

EXHIBITIONS

Open to all forms of relief printmaking. The work of members and non-members is subject to selection. Sending-in days are usually in summer and details may be obtained from the Secretary.

MEMBERSHIP

Applications for membership are considered from those who have had their work selected and hung in at least three different exhibitions organised by the SWE. Applicants are required to submit a portfolio of work and are elected on merit.

For information on courses/workshops, contact:
Kate Dicker
6 Rosewarne Court, Hyde Street, Winchester, Hants SO23 7HL
Tel: 01962 869617

Other correspondence to:
Geri Waddington
Secretary SWE, 3 West Street, Oundle, Northants PE8 4EJ
Tel/fax: 01832 275028
email: g.waddington@dial.pipex.com

WEBSITE

www.woodengravers.co.uk

CURRENT AND RECENT BOOKS ON WOOD ENGRAVING

CURRENT PRACTICE

Simon Brett, *An Engraver's Globe: Wood Engraving World-wide in the Twenty-first Century.* London, Primrose Hill Press, 2002

Simon Brett, *Wood Engraving – How To Do It.* Second revised edition, London, Primrose Hill Press, 2000.

HISTORY

James Hamilton, *Wood Engraving and the Woodcut in Britain c.1890–1990.* London, Barrie and Jenkins, 1994.

Joanna Selborne, *British Wood Engraved Book Illustration, 1904–1940. A Break with Tradition.* Oxford University Press, 1998; paperback edition: The British Library, 2001.

BOOKS FEATURING WOOD ENGRAVING

The Society's own Christmas books, fine print and illustrated with wood engravings (see catalogue nos. 18 and 60), appear annually. They may be obtained from The Secretary, Geri Waddington (address opposite), who is also a bookseller, specialising in wood engraved illustrated books.

The Primrose Hill Press (UK) is the foremost current publisher of books featuring wood engravings or about the work of wood engravers. The Whittington and the Fleece Presses lead the fine print field. The Primrose Academy and the Barbarian Press (Canada) each publish a series of limited edition monographs, with the blocks printed from the wood and introductions by the artist.

VENUES 2003–2004

BANKSIDE GALLERY
48 Hopton Street
(next to Tate Modern)
London SE1 9JH
8 November – 30 November 2003

Telephone: 020 7928 7521

ABERYSTWYTH SCHOOL OF ART MUSEUM & ART GALLERY
University of Wales
Buarth Mawr
Aberystwyth SY23 1NG
8 December – 13 February 2004

Telephone: 01970 622460

YARROW GALLERY
Oundle Road
Glapthorne Road
Oundle PE8 4GH
27 February – 20 March 2004

Telephone: 01832 277170

FRAMES GALLERY
Victoria Street
Perth PH2 8LW
10 April – 1 May 2004

Telephone: 01738 631085

WOODEND BARN ARTS CENTRE
Burn o'Bennie
Banchory AB31 5QA
8 May – 29 May 2004

Telephone: 01330 825431

SHETLAND MUSEUM
Lower Hillhead
Lerwick
Shetland ZE1 0EL
4 June – 25 June 2004

Telephone: 01595 695057

PONTEFRACT MUSEUM
5 Salter Row
Pontefract
W. Yorks WF8 1BA
3 July – 7 August 2004

Telephone: 01977 722741

Please telephone to confirm before making long journeys, as changes are sometimes necessary.